# Collins

# 11+

# Non-Verbal Reasoning and Spatial Reasoning

## Support & Practice Workbook

T0340565

Peter Francis and Chris Pearse

Published by Collins
An imprint of HarperCollins*Publishers* Ltd
1 London Bridge Street
London SE1 9GF

HarperCollins*Publishers*
39/40 Mayor Street Upper
Dublin 1
D01 C9W8
Ireland

ISBN 978-0-00-856259-5

First published 2023

10 9 8 7 6 5 4 3

British Library Cataloguing in Publication Data.
A CIP record of this book is available from the British Library.
Publisher: Clare Souza
Authors: Peter Francis and Chris Pearse
Project Management: Richard Toms
Cover Design: Kevin Robbins and Sarah Duxbury
Inside Concept Design: Ian Wrigley
Typesetting: Jouve India Private Limited and Ian Wrigley
Production: Emma Wood

Published in collaboration with Teachitright.
Billy the Bookworm™ is the property of Teachitright Ltd.

Printed in the United Kingdom by Ashford Colour Ltd

# Contents

## Teachitright

This book has been published in collaboration with Teachitright, one of the most successful 11+ tuition companies in the South-East. Teachitright has supported thousands of pupils for both grammar school and independent school entry. It has tuition centres across the UK, including Berkshire, Buckinghamshire, Surrey and the West Midlands.

With considerable experience and knowledge, Teachitright has produced a range of books to support children through their 11+ journey for GL Assessment, CEM and many Common Entrance exams. The books have been written by qualified teachers, tested in the classroom with pupils, and adapted to ensure children are fully prepared and able to perform to the best of their ability.

Teachitright's unique mascot, Billy the Bookworm, helps to guide children through this book and gives helpful hints and tips along the way. We hope your child finds this book useful and informative and we wish them luck on their 11+ journey.

Teachitright holds a number of comprehensive revision courses and mock exams throughout the year. For more information, visit **www.teachitright.com**

This Non-Verbal Reasoning and Spatial Reasoning Support and Practice Workbook provides the perfect preparation for GL Assessment 11+, Common Pre-test and Common Entrance exams. It contains these question types:

- Classes Unlike

- Classes Alike

- Series

- Analogies

- Matrices (both 2 × 2 and 3 × 3)

- Horizontal and Vertical Codes

- Shape Completion

- Rotation

- Cubes and Nets

- Fold and Punch

- Block Counting

**How to Use this Book**

As this book is divided into 11 lessons that cover different question types, it can be used to focus on individual areas of development or to work through every topic. There are three main parts to each lesson:

**Learn:** An informative teaching section to help with the key points and techniques for that question type. It includes worked examples.

**Develop:** An opportunity to practise a task to continually build the key principles and techniques taught in the Learn section.

**Succeed:** Timed tests to help build confidence with non-verbal and spatial reasoning questions and time management.

The answer section gives detailed explanations to aid revision. There is also a glossary on page 104. It is important for children to understand the correct non-verbal reasoning vocabulary to help aid their knowledge.

At the back of the book, a **marking chart** (on page 118) and **progress grid** (on page 119) help to track your child's development throughout the topics and highlight strengths and weaknesses.

**This book does not contain any official GL Assessment questions and it is not endorsed by GL Assessment.**

**Our question types are based on those set by GL Assessment, but we cannot guarantee that your child's actual 11+ exam will contain the same question types or format as this book.**

## Key Strategies to Use in this Book

Throughout this book, children can apply specific strategies to help find the correct answers. These are summarised here:

- Using a process of elimination can reduce the number of feasible answer options. This is also a way of ensuring that all the answer options have been considered and a subtle difference between the figures hasn't been overlooked. This strategy is a particularly good approach for **analogies**.

- Going through a checklist of features can help to identify correct answers. For **classes alike** and **classes unlike** questions, this mnemonic provides a structured approach to finding the feature that might have changed between figures:

    **S**hape – Silly

    **P**osition – People

    **A**ngle – Always

    **N**umber – Need

    **S**ize – Soggy

    **S**hading – Socks


    **R**otation – Rotten

    **O**verlapping – Oranges

    **S**ymmetry – Smell

- In **matrices**, **series**, **shape completion** or **fold and punch** questions, it may help to draw figures in the empty box or in a blank space to help visualise the answer.

- When tackling **horizontal and vertical code** questions, it might not be necessary to work out the code for every single letter and this could save valuable time.

- When dealing with **nets**, it is helpful to work out which faces will lie opposite each other when it is folded into a cube. The orientation of the different shapes on the faces should also be taken into consideration when working out the answer.

- When solving **rotation** questions, it may help to turn the page to see how a figure will look in a different orientation.

- In **block counting** questions, writing the number of blocks in each section of the diagram can avoid them being recounted or miscounted.

- Completing questions carefully and within a time limit is a key skill when solving non-verbal and spatial reasoning questions. Answering questions in under 30 seconds is always a good benchmark.

## Online Video Tutorial

An online video tutorial to help with techniques is available at
**www.collins.co.uk/11plusresources**

**THIS PAGE HAS DELIBERATELY
BEEN LEFT BLANK**

# LESSON I:

# CLASSES UNLIKE

Look out for Billy's tips and hints.

# LEARN

This 2D question type involves spotting the figure that is most unlike the others in a set. It is often easier to group four figures together that have something in common, as this then leaves the one figure that is different from all the others.

## Warm-up task

To help improve your observation skills, choose five everyday items of the same kind and try to find an odd one out. Below are three examples to get you started and to help you think about how things can be grouped together to leave an odd one out. Look at sizes, shapes, colours and anything else that might make one item different from another.

①

The 2p coin could be the odd one out because of the colour.

②

The American football could be the odd one out because it is not round.

③

The orange pencil on the right could be the odd one out because it is turned upside down.

## Thinking about more than one feature of a 2D figure

For the more challenging questions, you will need to consider more than one feature. The answer might be to do with how the features of a figure are linked together. For example, you might need to count the number of sides or corners of shapes. In the example below, there are twice as many sides on the outer shape as there are small triangles inside. However, if you add up the sides on the 3 triangles, you have 9 sides.

Linking features (sometimes called elements or properties) in figures is something you will need to do in the Succeed section later in this lesson. Remember to think about how the features work together.

## Worked example

Find the figure that is most unlike the others.

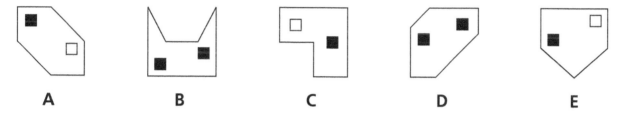

|   A   |   B   |   C   |   D   |   E   |

## Method

(1)  Firstly, look at each figure and its features. Work from left to right to ensure you don't miss any options.

(2)  Identify whether any of the figures have any common features. For example, here you might notice that they all have small squares inside the larger outer shape. However, some are pairs of white and black squares and some are pairs of black squares, so you can't use this to find the odd one out.

(3)  Look at another part of the figures. The outer shapes all look different and often it is worth counting how many sides the shapes have. To avoid counting the same side again, it is helpful to place a line on each one as shown below, and then to write the number of sides above each shape to identify if there are any patterns.

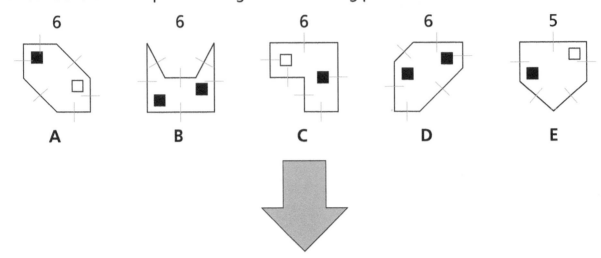

| 6 | 6 | 6 | 6 | 5 |
|---|---|---|---|---|
| A | B | C | D | E |

(4)  If you count the sides on each outer shape, you will find that E has 5 sides while the rest of the shapes all have 6 sides. So, **E** is the figure that is most unlike the others.

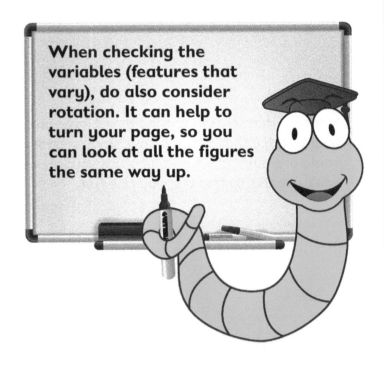

**When checking the variables (features that vary), do also consider rotation. It can help to turn your page, so you can look at all the figures the same way up.**

# DEVELOP

Here are some to try for yourself.

For each question, circle the letter under the figure that is most unlike the others.

   **A**         **B**         **C**         **D**         **E**

   **A**         **B**         **C**         **D**         **E**

   **A**         **B**         **C**         **D**         **E**

   **A**         **B**         **C**         **D**         **E**

   **A**         **B**         **C**         **D**         **E**

# SUCCEED

For each question, circle the letter under the figure that is most unlike the others.

**Example**

A      B      C      D      E

Answer: **D**. The white circle in each figure does not overlap a corner of the large shape.

**Now start the clock and do as many of these 15 questions as you can in 6 minutes.**

①

    A      B      C      D      E

②

    A      B      C      D      E

③

    A      B      C      D      E

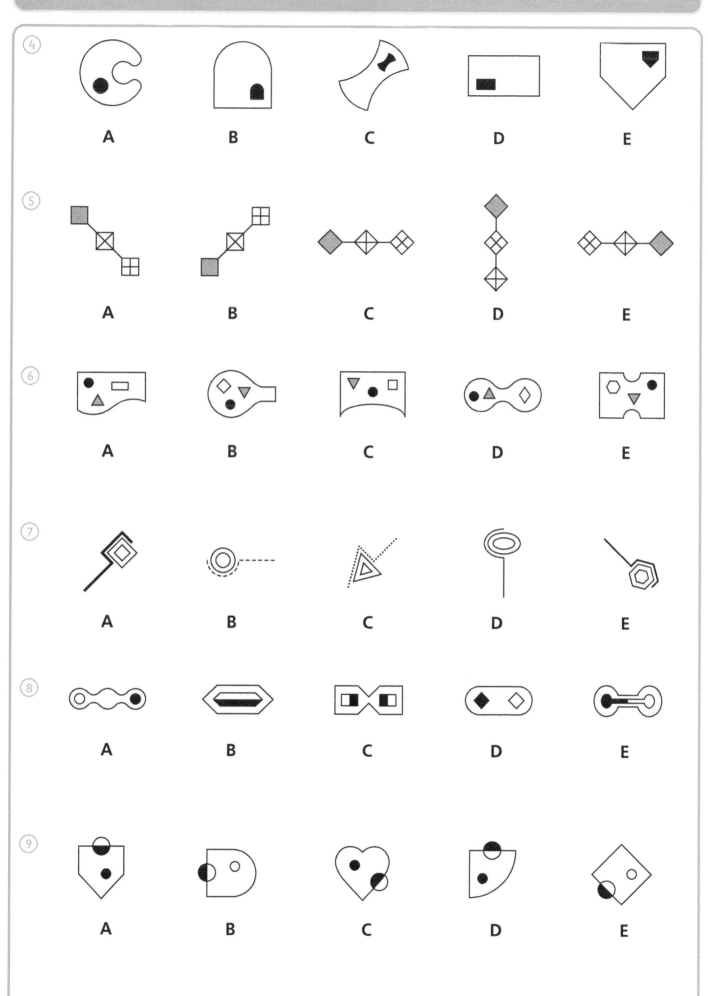

(4)

A     B     C     D     E

(5)

A     B     C     D     E

(6)

A     B     C     D     E

(7)

A     B     C     D     E

(8)

A     B     C     D     E

(9)

A     B     C     D     E

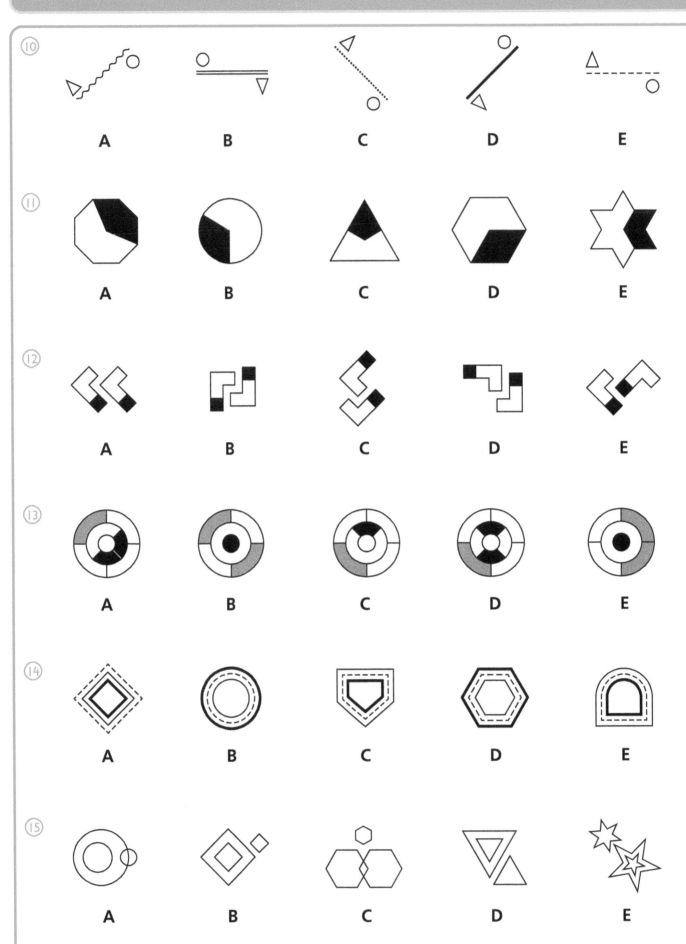

10.   A   B   C   D   E

11.   A   B   C   D   E

12.   A   B   C   D   E

13.   A   B   C   D   E

14.   A   B   C   D   E

15.   A   B   C   D   E

# LESSON 2:

# CLASSES ALIKE

Look out for Billy's tips and hints.

# LEARN

This question type is about finding a figure that fits with another group of images. You will need to compare figures and spot the similarities and differences between them. The answer will have something in common with the figures on the left that the other options do not. Recalling the features within SPANSS ROS (the mnemonic explained on page 7) will help to find the similarities between the images.

## Worked example

Circle the letter under the figure that is most similar to the figures to the left of the vertical line.

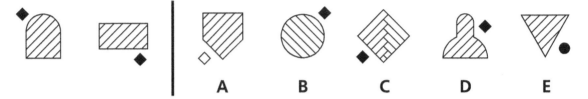

## Method

(1)   First, look at the figures on the left and decide what they have in common. You will notice that the large shapes have hatched shading going diagonally right to left. Now you can eliminate the options that don't have this common variable. Options B and C can be ruled out.

(2)   Sometimes you will only need to look at one element. If you are still left with more than one possible answer, look for other common traits in the figures on the left. Each figure contains a black square. This allows A and E to be eliminated.

(3)   Repeat this process until you have one answer left – that leaves **D**.

## Warm-up task

*Spot the change*

This is a simple but fun game to play with a family member or friend. One player draws a picture of an object or perhaps a person's face. Give it to the other player and they secretly add an additional feature, such as eyelashes. Then you have to spot the feature that has been added to the picture.

# DEVELOP

Here are some to try for yourself.

For each question, circle the letter under the figure that is most similar to the figures to the left of the vertical line.

  |

     **A**       **B**       **C**       **D**       **E**

(2)

  |

     **A**       **B**       **C**       **D**       **E**

(3)

  |

     **A**       **B**       **C**       **D**       **E**

(4)

   |       

     **A**       **B**       **C**       **D**       **E**

(5)

   |

     **A**       **B**       **C**       **D**       **E**

## SUCCEED

For each question, circle the option that is most similar to the figures to the left of the vertical line.

**Example**

A     B     C     D     E

Answer: **A.** The figure contains hatched shading running in the same diagonal direction and has a white square shape outside the hatched shape.

**Now start the clock and do as many of these 15 questions as you can in 6 minutes.**

①

A     B     C     D     E

②

A     B     C     D     E

③

A     B     C     D     E

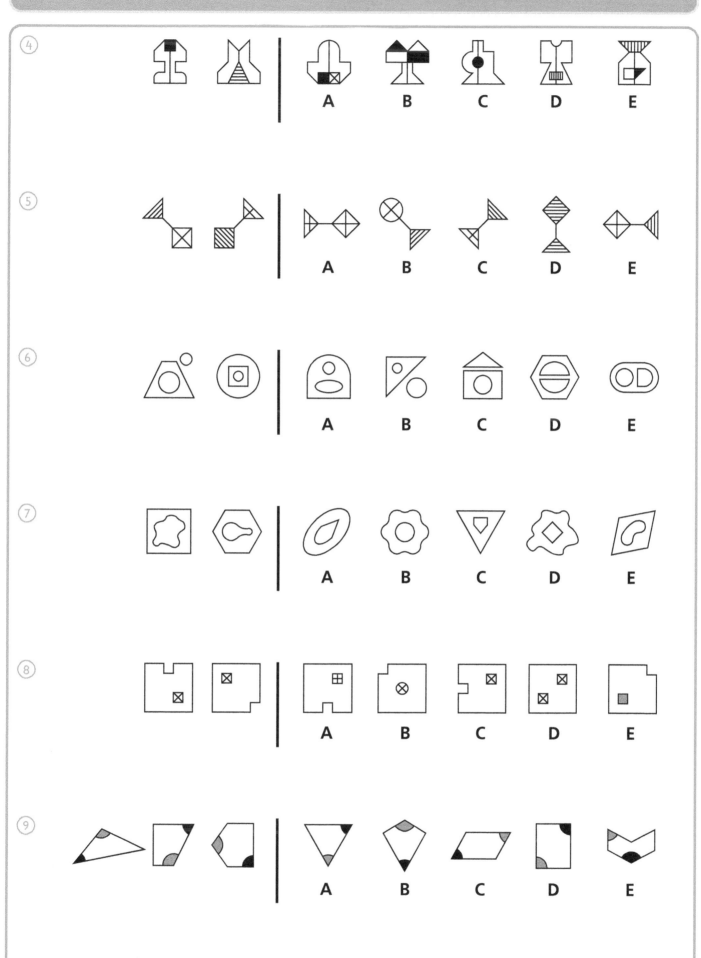

④

A  B  C  D  E

⑤

A  B  C  D  E

⑥

A  B  C  D  E

⑦

A  B  C  D  E

⑧

A  B  C  D  E

⑨

A  B  C  D  E

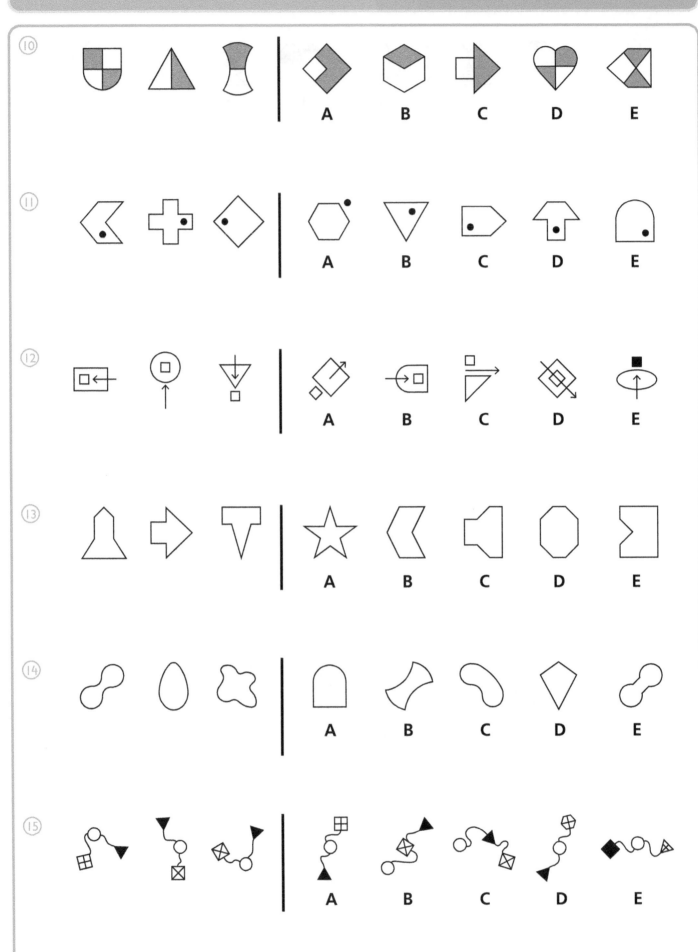

# LESSON 3:

## SERIES

Look out for Billy's tips and hints.

# LEARN

This question type involves completing a series of figures by deciding which answer option best completes the series. Look at how the sequence is created and in which direction the series is changing. For example, if the first box is empty, then work backwards to establish the pattern. If one of the middle boxes is empty, use the figures on either side of the empty box.

**Warm-up task**

To help get you warmed up, here is a simple series that needs completing. Find the missing figure to go in the empty box.

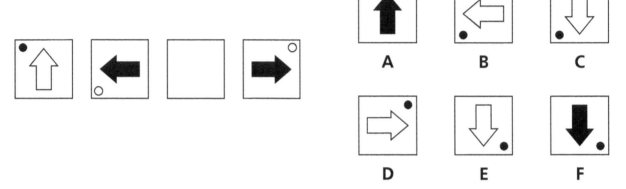

It can help to look at one feature at a time if the question is complex. Often questions will involve shapes rotating, and so it is important to know the difference between clockwise and anti-clockwise. Drawing a simple arrow can remind you in which direction the shape is moving.

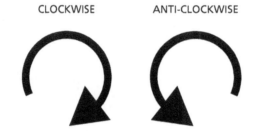

Drawing part of the shapes that you think should go in the empty box before looking at the answer options can be useful for these questions. You will have a limited period of time to answer each question in the actual 11+ exam. Therefore do not draw the entire figure as this will waste time.

## Worked example

Select the answer option that would complete the series.

A          B          C

D          E          F

(1) First decide in which direction the series is working. As the third box is empty, look at the first two boxes and identify how the figures change. In the example above, the triangle rotates anti-clockwise 90°. Therefore, the triangle in the empty box will need to be pointing downwards. So, eliminate answer options A, B and D.

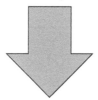

(2) The triangles also alternate between black and white. The triangle in the empty box will need to be white, so eliminate option F, leaving possible options C and E.

(3) Next, look at the other feature in the pattern; the small circles. They alternate between black and white so the empty box will need to have a black circle. Options C and E both have a black circle, so now you will have to consider where they are positioned. The circles move anti-clockwise around the box. From the sequence we can see the black circle in the empty box will need to be placed in the bottom right corner. In option C the circle is on the left, so the answer must be **E**.

You can create your own series using paper and pencil. Ask a friend or family member to complete it.

# DEVELOP

In each question, select the answer option that would complete the series.

①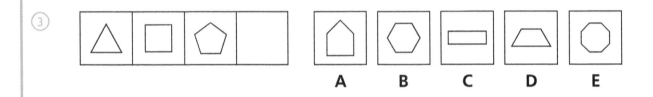

② 

③ 

④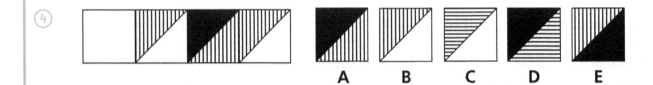

## SUCCEED

In each question, select the answer option that would complete the series.

**Example**

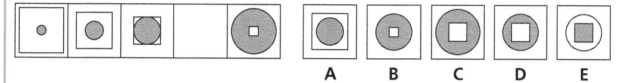

Answer: **D**. The white square shrinks and the grey circle grows in size.

**Now start the clock and do as many of these 15 questions as you can in 6 minutes.**

①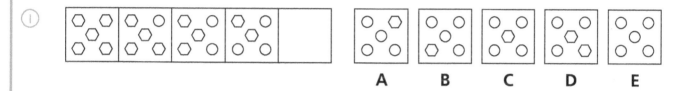

②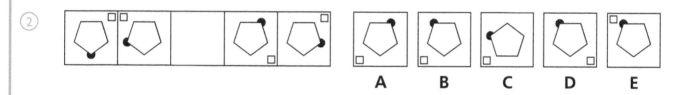

③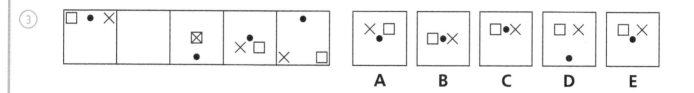

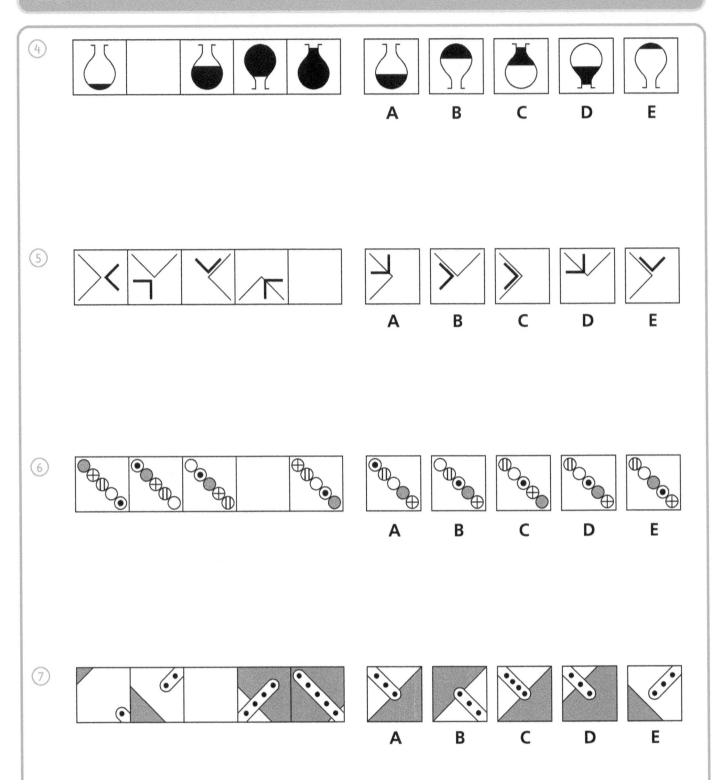

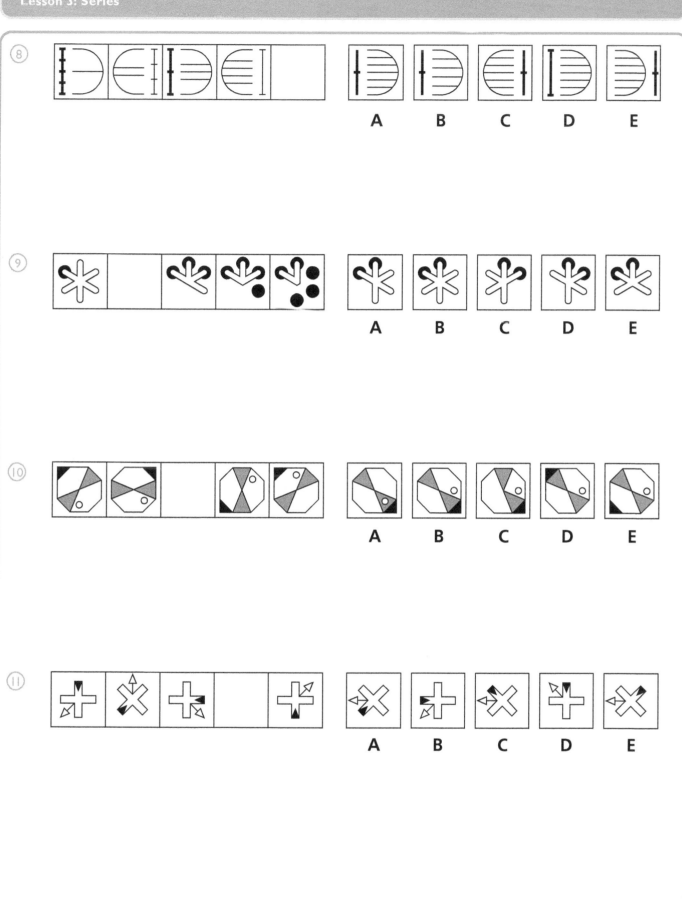

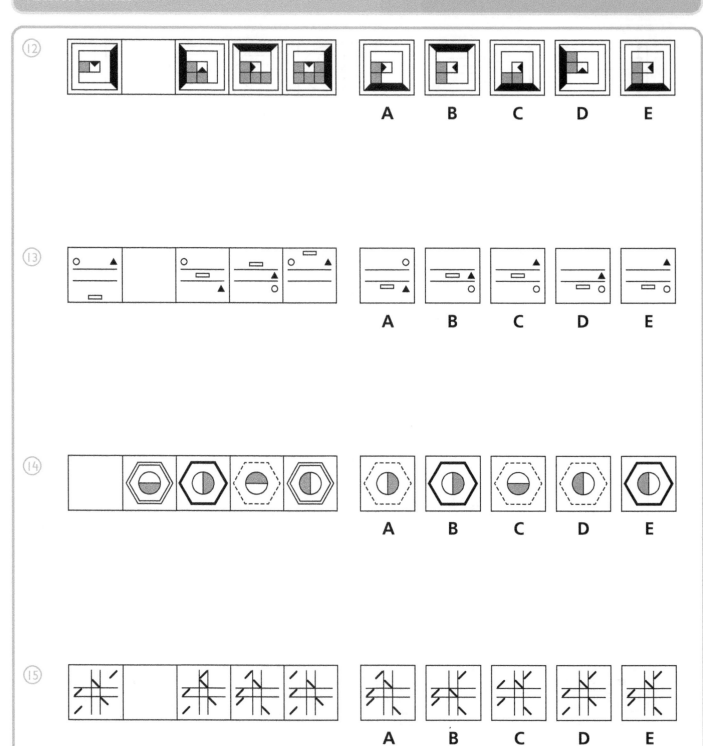

# LESSON 4:

## ANALOGIES

Look out for Billy's tips and hints.

# LEARN

In this question type you need to spot a relationship between two figures. Once you've discovered what has changed in the first figure to make the second figure, you then apply the same relationship to make another pair of figures. This question type can easily be created in your home with everyday objects, as with classes unlike questions in the first lesson.

An example in words might help you understand this more easily – for example, 'Kitten is to Cat as Puppy is to . . . .?' Here the first item is a baby animal and the second item is that baby animal grown up. The third item is another baby animal and so you have to think of what animal it might become when grown up – Dog.

## Warm-up task

Think about what has changed between the first and second items, then apply this change on the third item to make the fourth item. Draw what the fourth item should be in the empty box.

is to ⸻ as ⸻ is to

| A | B | C | D |

is to ⸻ as ⸻ is to

| A | B | C | D |

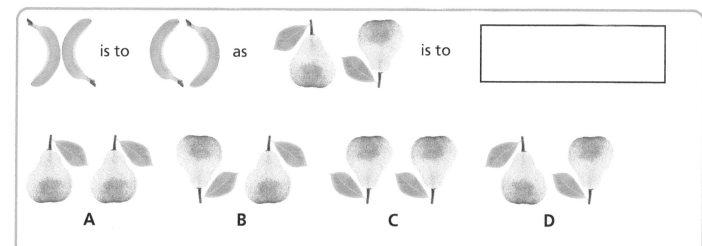

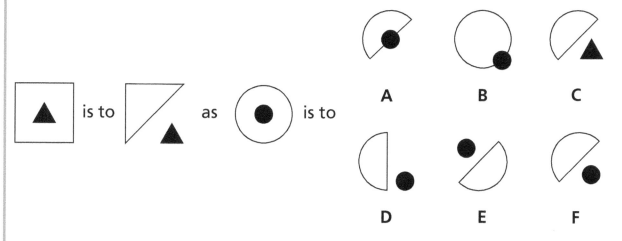

More complex analogies may have more than one change between each pair. If more than one change is taking place, use each change to rule out some answer options. At first glance, sometimes the pairs can seem as though each figure is completely different from the first. All you need to do is spot which changes have been made between the figures in each pair. Take one feature at a time when the question looks difficult.

**Worked example**

**Method**

(1)   The first shape has a small black triangle inside a square. In the second figure the black triangle has moved to the bottom right and the square has become a right-angled triangle (or you could simply say that the square has been halved diagonally).

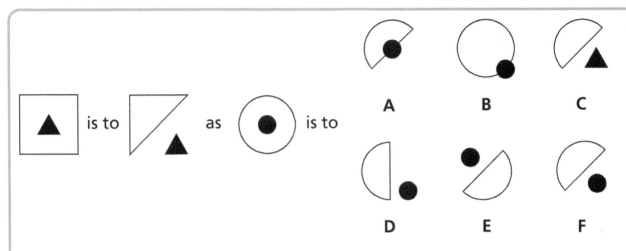

(2)    Next, the third figure contains a small black circle inside a larger circle. Look for any answer options which don't contain the small black circle. Cross out C.

(3)    The larger circle must be halved diagonally to create a semi-circle. So, B can be eliminated. The semi-circle must appear in the top left corner. So, options D and E can also be ruled out.

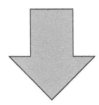

(4)    This only leaves options A and F. Only one of these shapes has the black circle in the correct position. Therefore, **F** is the option which completes the analogy in the best possible way.

**It is important to know your degrees when tackling analogies. Try to turn this book 45°, 90°, 135°, 180°, 225°, 270°, 315° and 360°.**

# DEVELOP

Look at the figures in each question. Work out how the first figure has been changed into the second, then identify how the third figure would change if it were altered in the same way. Circle the letter below the correct answer option.

①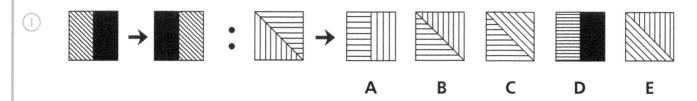

A     B     C     D     E

②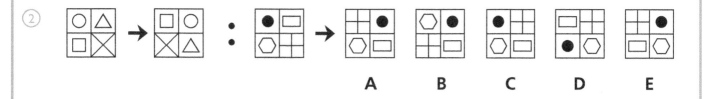

A     B     C     D     E

③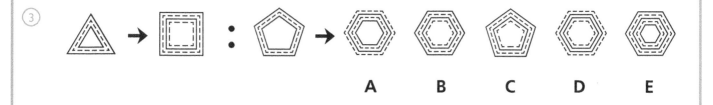

A     B     C     D     E

④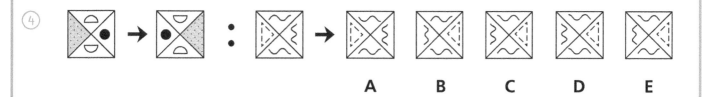

A     B     C     D     E

# SUCCEED

Look at the figures in each question. Work out how the first figure has been changed into the second, then identify how the third figure would change if it were altered in the same way. Circle the letter below the correct answer option.

**Example**

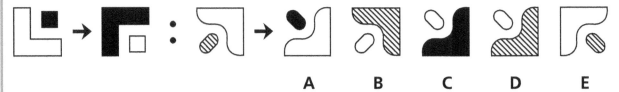

Answer: **D**. The figure rotates 90° clockwise and the shapes swap shading.

**Now start the clock and do as many of these 15 questions as you can in 6 minutes.**

①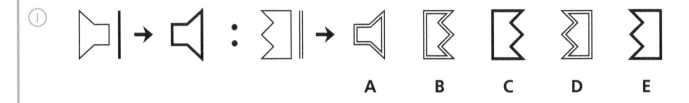

②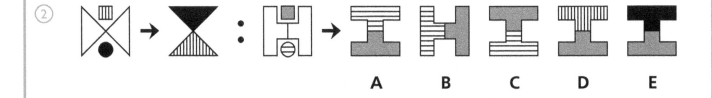

③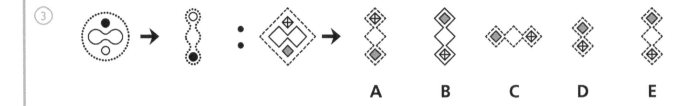

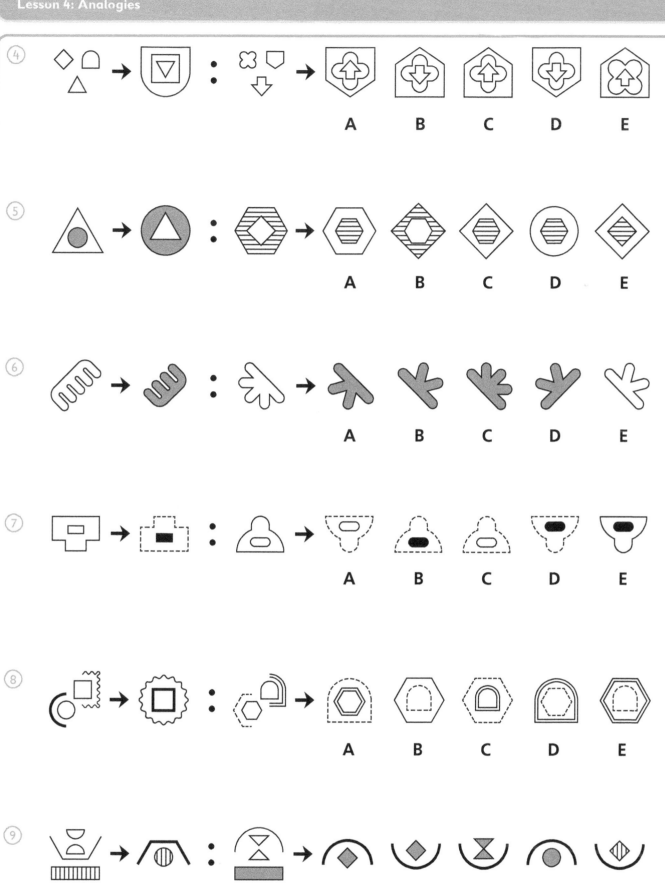

④ A    B    C    D    E

⑤ A    B    C    D    E

⑥ A    B    C    D    E

⑦ A    B    C    D    E

⑧ A    B    C    D    E

⑨ A    B    C    D    E

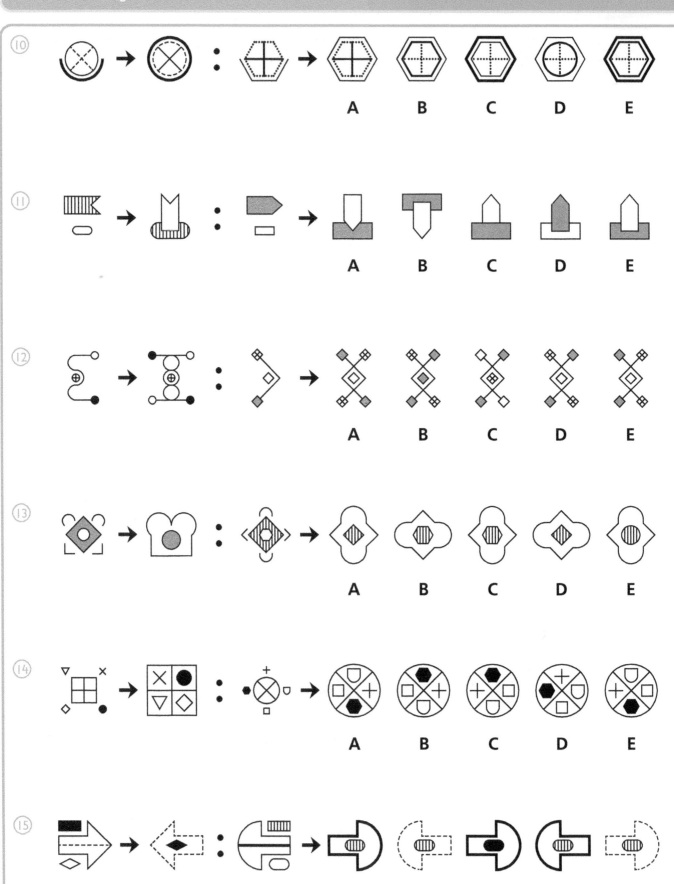

# LESSON 5:

# MATRICES

Look out for **Billy's** tips and hints.

# LEARN

In these questions you need to find out which answer option fits in the empty box of the grid. The grids can be 2 × 2 or 3 × 3. The key skill is to identify the pattern, changes or similarities. First you need to establish how the pattern is arranged, whether it is in rows, columns or both. Look carefully at the completed rows or columns (those without the empty square). Sometimes, a quick glance will reveal how the grid is put together. In other questions you will need to study the grid more closely. Matrices with three rows and columns often include diagonal patterns.

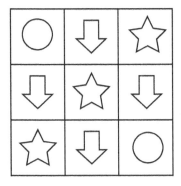

**Worked example**

In the grid on the left, one of the small squares has been left empty. Select one of the five figures on the right to best fit into the empty square.

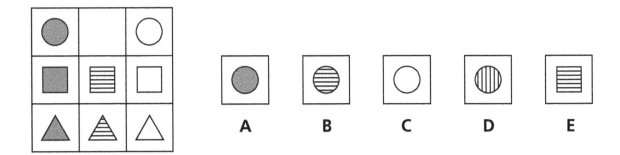

**Method**

(1) In the example above, it is clear that the pattern uses both columns and rows. The columns determine the shading of the shapes and the rows determine the 2D shape.

(2)   Now look at the features you would expect from the empty square. The shape will be a circle. This enables you to eliminate option E.

(3)   The shading in the middle column will have horizontal shading. This allows you to eliminate options A, C and D.

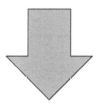

(4)   Therefore the answer is **B**.

> Matrices can have several different variations. It is important you check all the possibilities. These include a Latin square format (a grid where each symbol occurs once in each row and once in each column). Other differences include combining columns to make a figure in another column. Furthermore, these grids can be reflections and need a good knowledge of mirroring.

**Warm-up task**

*Follow the pattern*

Being able to follow a pattern over more than one row is a further variation. Can you work out the pattern in the grid below?

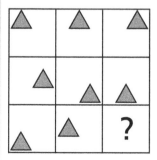

# DEVELOP

Look at the following matrices. For each one, select the correct figure from the answer options to complete the grid.

①

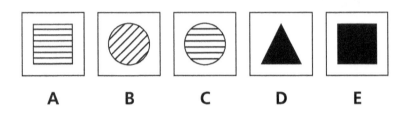

A     B     C     D     E

②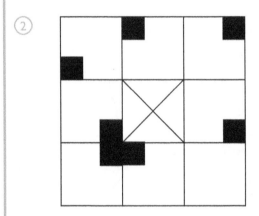

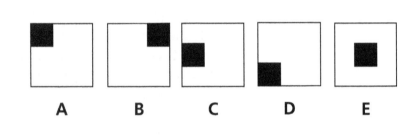

A     B     C     D     E

③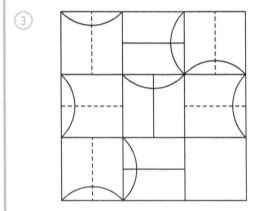

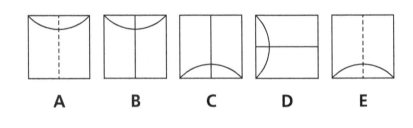

A     B     C     D     E

(4)

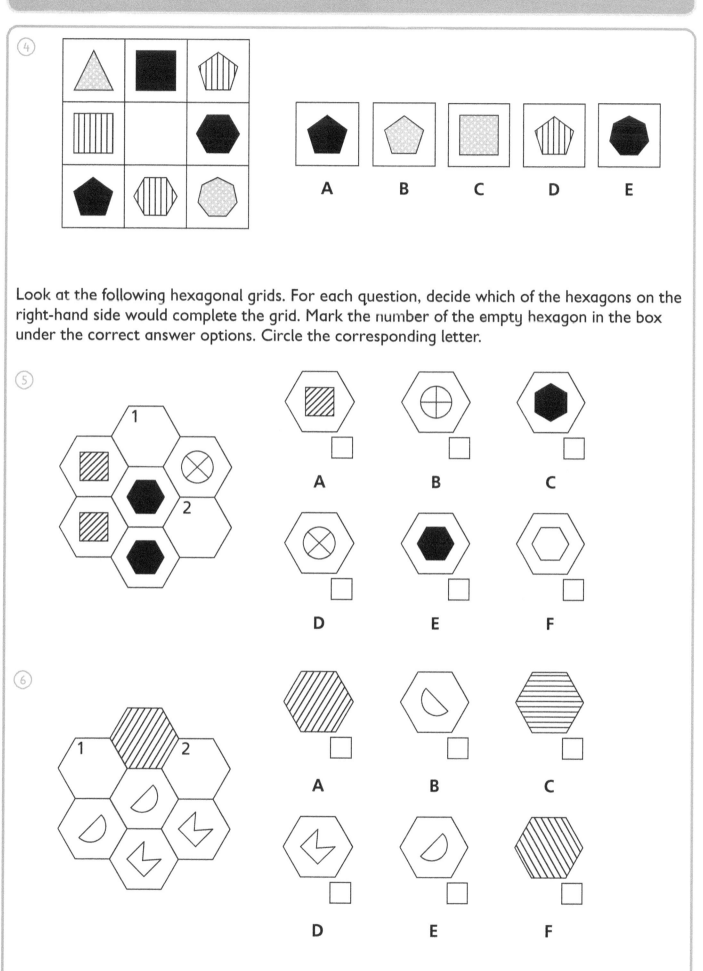

Look at the following hexagonal grids. For each question, decide which of the hexagons on the right-hand side would complete the grid. Mark the number of the empty hexagon in the box under the correct answer options. Circle the corresponding letter.

(5)

A    B    C

D    E    F

(6)

A    B    C

D    E    F

## SUCCEED

Look at the following matrices. For each one, select the correct figure from the answer options to complete the grid. Circle the corresponding letter.

**Example:**

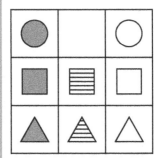

A             B             C             D             E

Answer: **B**. The shapes are the same in rows and the shading is the same in columns.

**Now start the clock and do as many of these 15 questions as you can in 6 minutes.**

① 
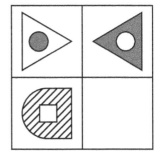

A             B             C             D             E

② 
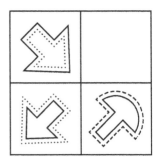

A             B             C             D             E

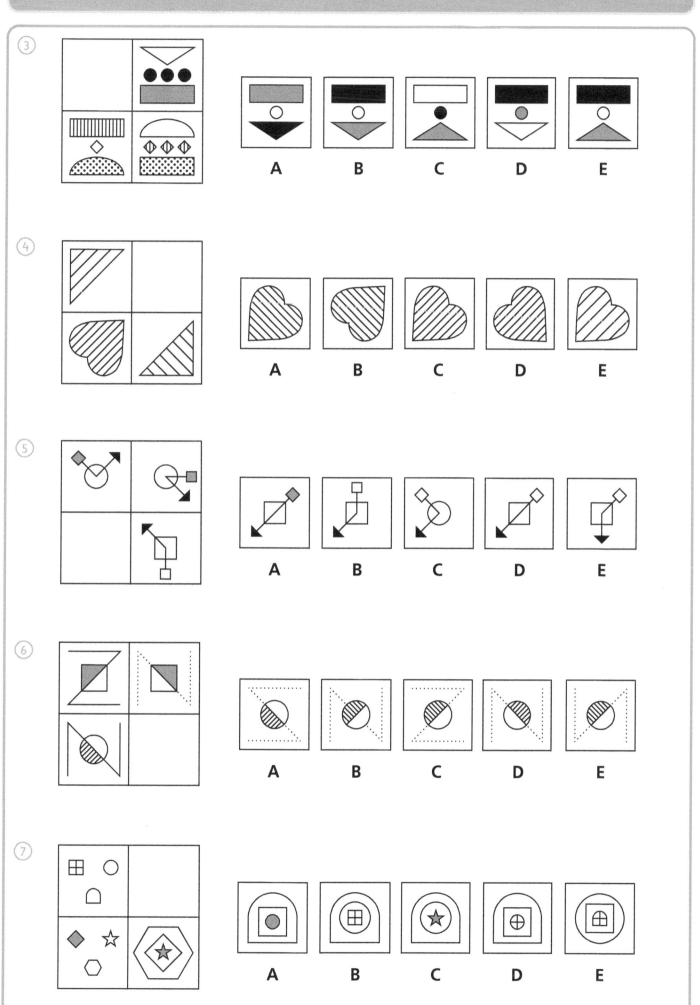

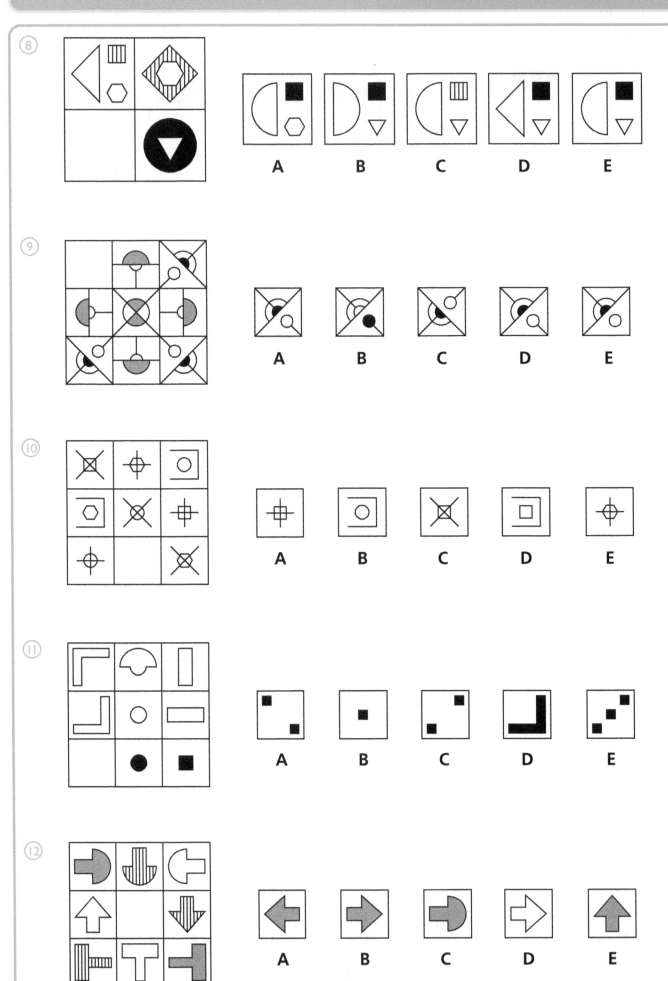

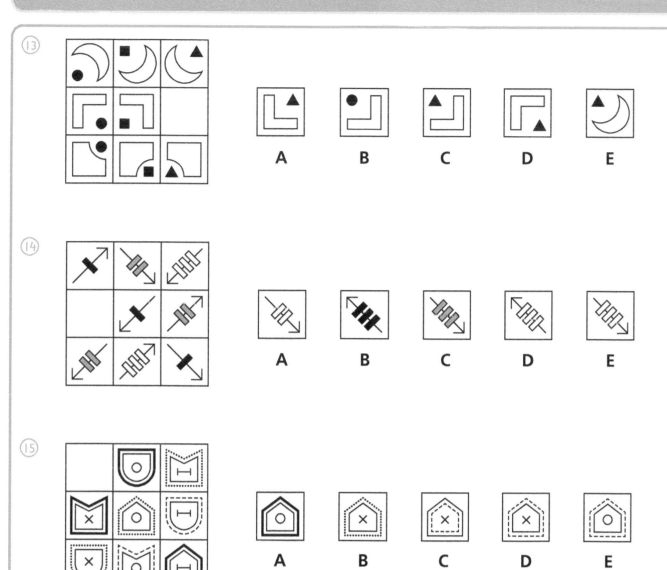

**THIS PAGE HAS DELIBERATELY
BEEN LEFT BLANK**

# LESSON 6:

# HORIZONTAL AND VERTICAL CODES

Look out for Billy's tips and hints.

# LEARN

In these questions you need to be like a detective to work out what each letter of a code represents using the clues. The strategies outlined on page 7 are very important here.

On the left, you will be given a set of diagrams, set horizontally or vertically, that have codes. You will need to find the correct code for the 'test shape' given to the right.

Look at the first letter in each code given on the left and identify those that are the same. Remember that each letter stands for a particular feature in the diagram. The first letter represents one feature of the diagram, the second letter stands for another, and so on.

## Worked example

This question has some figures on the left with code letters to describe them. Work out what the code letters stand for. Use this knowledge to work out which code describes the shape that is on its own.

## Method

(1) In the example above, the two Fs stand for the outside shape. Both are squares. Therefore, G represents the hexagon and this is the first letter of the code we are looking for. Eliminate options B and C, which both begin with an F.

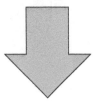

(2) Move to the second letter in the given codes and establish what the diagrams coded by the letter Y have in common. These diagrams have a small grey-shaded shape inside. This suggests that the test shape requires an X for the unshaded shape that is divided into quarters. Option A can be ruled out based on the second letter.

(3)   The third letter in the given codes still needs to be solved as two options remain (D and E). The two diagrams coded by an R contain a circle in the middle. This indicates that S stands for a small square as seen in the diagram for code FYS. The S is needed for the small square in the test shape and so this means that the answer must be **D** (code GXS).

## Warm-up task

*Create your own*

Creating your own code question can be an enjoyable and educational activity. You can test it out on a friend or a family member.

First decide if you are making a two- or a three-letter coded question. When creating your own code questions, try to consider the key properties that could be changed. These might include the line style, number of shapes, reflected figures or size of the shapes.

Here is an example of a two-lettered horizontal code. Try to work it out.

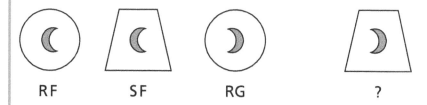

| RF | SF | RG | ? |

Be careful! Sometimes it can be easy to get confused when a right-hand letter represents something on the left of the diagram and a left-hand letter relates to something on the right.

# DEVELOP

Now try these.

Each of the figures on the left have a code. Work out what the letters of the code mean and then choose the correct code for the figure given to the right.

①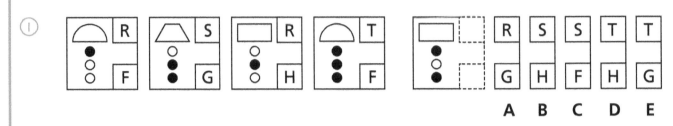

A   B   C   D   E

②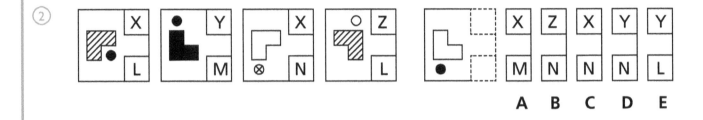

A   B   C   D   E

③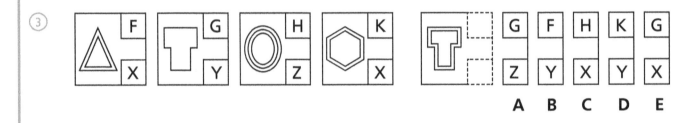

A   B   C   D   E

④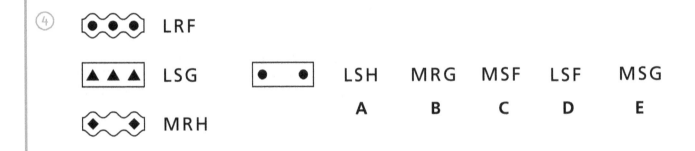

|  | LSH | MRG | MSF | LSF | MSG |
|---|---|---|---|---|---|
|  | A | B | C | D | E |

⑤

|  | XGN | YFL | YGL | XFM | XGM |
|---|---|---|---|---|---|
|  | A | B | C | D | E |

## SUCCEED

Each of the figures on the left have a code. Work out what the letters of the code mean and then choose the correct code for the figure given to the right.

**Example**

   FXR

   GYR              GYS    FYR    FXS    GXS    GXR

                                                             A      B      C      D      E

    FYS

Answer: **A**. FG stands for the large shape, XY stands for the shading of the small shape and RS stands for the type of small shape.

**Now start the clock and do as many of these 15 questions as you can in 7½ minutes.**

①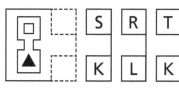

                                                          A    B    C    D    E

②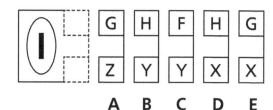

                                                           A    B    C    D    E

③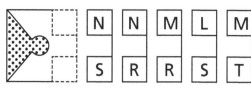

                                                           A    B    C    D    E

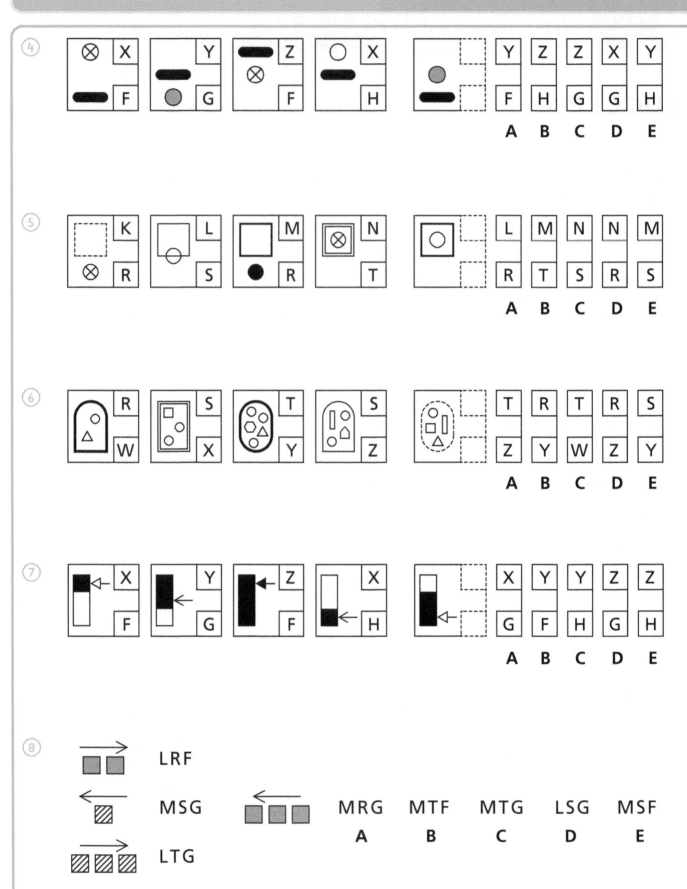

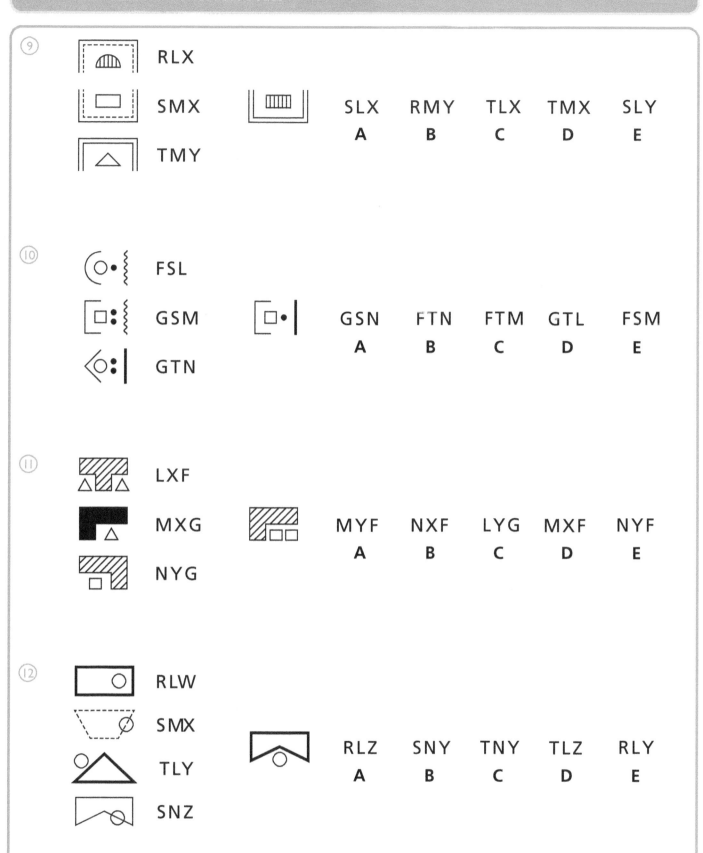

⑨

RLX

SMX

TMY

| | SLX | RMY | TLX | TMX | SLY |
|---|-----|-----|-----|-----|-----|
| | **A** | **B** | **C** | **D** | **E** |

⑩

FSL

GSM

GTN

| | GSN | FTN | FTM | GTL | FSM |
|---|-----|-----|-----|-----|-----|
| | **A** | **B** | **C** | **D** | **E** |

⑪

LXF

MXG

NYG

| | MYF | NXF | LYG | MXF | NYF |
|---|-----|-----|-----|-----|-----|
| | **A** | **B** | **C** | **D** | **E** |

⑫

RLW

SMX

TLY

SNZ

| | RLZ | SNY | TNY | TLZ | RLY |
|---|-----|-----|-----|-----|-----|
| | **A** | **B** | **C** | **D** | **E** |

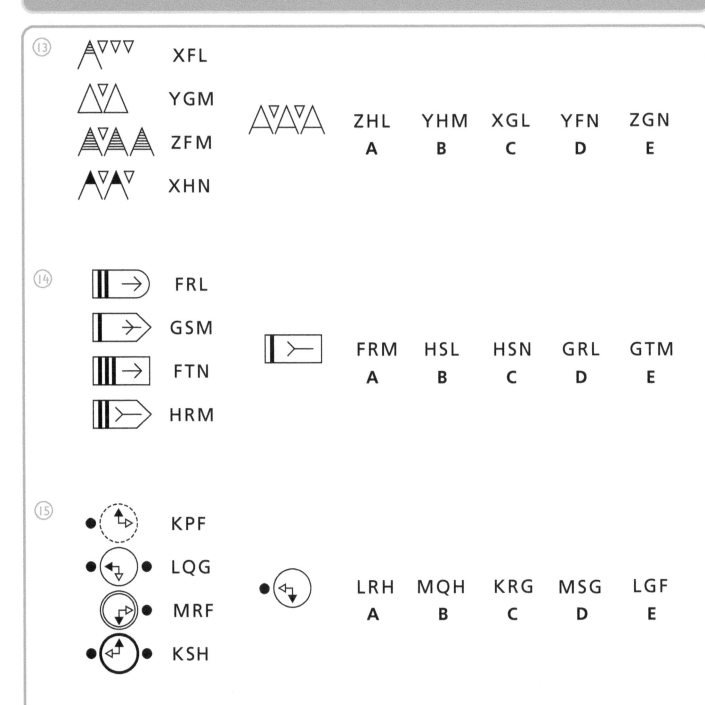

⑬

XFL

YGM

ZFM

XHN

| | ZHL | YHM | XGL | YFN | ZGN |
|---|-----|-----|-----|-----|-----|
| | A | B | C | D | E |

⑭

FRL

GSM

FTN

HRM

| | FRM | HSL | HSN | GRL | GTM |
|---|-----|-----|-----|-----|-----|
| | A | B | C | D | E |

⑮

KPF

LQG

MRF

KSH

| | LRH | MQH | KRG | MSG | LGF |
|---|-----|-----|-----|-----|-----|
| | A | B | C | D | E |

# LESSON 7:

# SHAPE COMPLETION

# LEARN

Shape completion questions require keen visualisation skills. These jigsaw-like questions require you to find the piece or pieces that, when combined with the part-shape in front of the plus symbol, form the figure on the far left.

Let's look at a worked example. In this particular example, the right-hand figures do not need to be rotated/moved at all to create the left-hand shape.

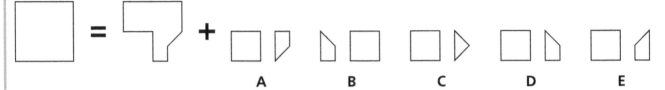

## Method

(1)    Think about the figure on the left. What is distinctive or particularly noticeable about it? For example, how many sides or corners does it have? Are the sides straight or curved? What angles does the figure have? Do any parts stick out? Compare it with the part-shape to its right. Decide which pieces are missing in the part-shape.

(2)    If completing a paper-based test, you can shade in the missing parts. This will help you to see the whole figure and help to match your shaded areas to the answer options. This is more difficult on-screen, but it can help you to visualise the whole figure.

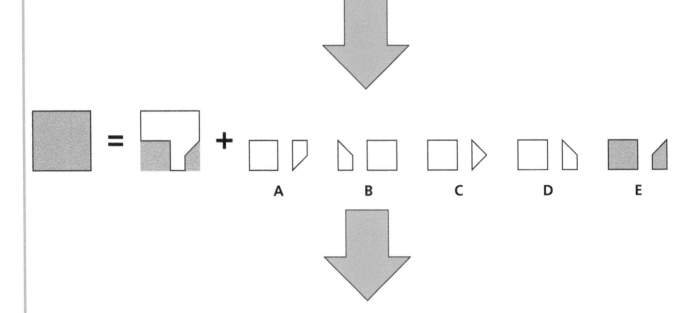

(3)     If there are two missing pieces, it's a good idea to focus on one at a time. Then eliminate any answer options that don't contain the matching piece. Also, consider if the pieces are on the right or left of the figure.

(4)     Focus on the next piece and ensure it makes the whole figure on the left.

(5)     Finally, imagine the pieces together and the complete figure. The answer to this example question is **E**.

Be aware that sometimes in this question type, the shapes on the right-hand side may need to be rotated before joining with the figure on the left.

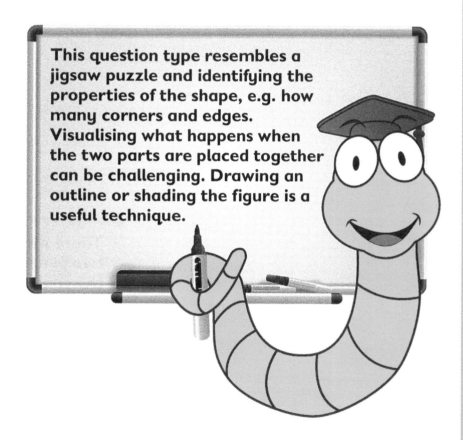

This question type resembles a jigsaw puzzle and identifying the properties of the shape, e.g. how many corners and edges. Visualising what happens when the two parts are placed together can be challenging. Drawing an outline or shading the figure is a useful technique.

## Fun task

A variety of fun games can help you improve your ability to link shapes together to form the whole. One enjoyable video game is *Tetris*. Jigsaw puzzles can also help with linking shapes together and seeing how the parts form the whole image. Many people have wooden puzzles that can be bought from craft fairs or a local gift shop. These are excellent for visualising spaces and deciding which block fits where.

You could create your own puzzle or ask someone to put a puzzle together. To make it more complex, cut out small pieces or make sure the pieces are small.

There may be one or two pieces missing from the complete shape. Sometimes the pieces need rotating to fit to the target shape but this is not always the case.

# DEVELOP

Look at the first figure on the left. Which of the answer options should be added to the first figure on the right to form the figure on the left? Circle the letter for the correct answer.

①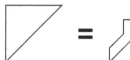

   A         B         C         D         E

②

   A         B         C         D         E

③

   A         B         C         D         E

④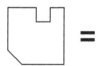

   A         B         C         D         E

⑤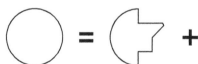

   A         B         C         D         E

**SUCCEED**

Look at the first figure on the left. Which of the answer options should be added to the first figure on the right to form the figure on the left? Circle the letter for the correct answer.

**Example**

□ = M + ▽  ▽  ▽  ▽  □

          A       B       C       D       E

Answer: **D**

**Now start the clock and do as many of these 15 questions as you can in 6 minutes.**

① ◇ = ◁ + △ ▷ ⬢ ⬡ ⬡

              A       B       C       D       E

② ⬡ = ⬡ + ⬡ ⬡ ⬡ ⬡ ⬡

              A       B       C       D       E

③ ▷ = ⊏ + ⬠ ⬠ ⬠ ⬠ ⬠

              A       B       C       D       E

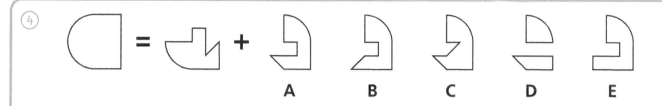

④    =    +    A    B    C    D    E

⑤    =    +    A    B    C    D    E

⑥    =    +    A    B    C    D    E

⑦    =    +    A    B    C    D    E

⑧    =    +    A    B    C    D    E

⑨    =    +    A    B    C    D    E

⑩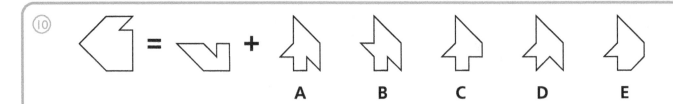

A     B     C     D     E

⑪ 

A     B     C     D     E

⑫ 

A     B     C     D     E

⑬ 

A     B     C     D     E

⑭ 

A     B     C     D     E

⑮ 

A     B     C     D     E

# LESSON 8:

# ROTATION

Look out for Billy's tips and hints.

# LEARN

Rotation involves an object turning around its centre or around another point. There are different ways shapes can rotate and they will often look different afterwards. If you find these questions challenging, try turning the page to help you work out what is happening. This is a common thing to do when using a map to ensure you have the correct direction.

In rotation questions, it is important to recognise that the size, shape and shading of the original figure will not change in the rotated image. However, the orientation of the figure's features will depend on the degree of rotation.

Note that figures may be rotated as part of other question types covered in this book, for example analogies, series and matrices.

**Worked example**

Choose the figure on the right that is a rotation of the figure on the left.

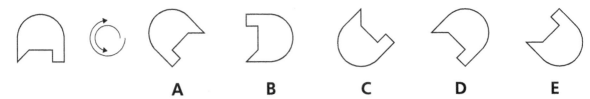

A       B       C       D       E

**Method**

(1)   First look at the features of the shape on the left that is being rotated. This should make it easier to identify the answer. The shape has a distinct triangle and square sticking out at the bottom. Use these features as 'handles' for the rotation to help you visualise where they will end up.

(2)   It is important not to confuse rotation with reflection. The image in figure A is a reflection of the shape on the left, not a rotation. This option can therefore be eliminated.

(3)   B, C and E are also reflections. The answer is therefore **D**.

Look for shading (especially hatched shading) that can give you a clue to the direction of rotation. Focusing on angles on a line, and shapes within other figures, can give a clue to the rotated position of larger figures.

## Warm-up task

*Different degrees*

Practising rotating shapes through different degrees can help you to develop the skills for these questions. The table below shows shapes that will be rotated through different degrees. See if you can accurately draw the shape according to the degrees it will be rotated **clockwise**.

| Shape | Rotated 45° | Rotated 90° | Rotated 135° | Rotated 180° |
|---|---|---|---|---|
| | | | | |
| | | | | |
| | | | | |
| | | | | |

# DEVELOP

Now try these.

Choose the figure on the right that is a rotation of the figure on the left.

①

                    A             B           C           D           E

②

                    A             B           C           D           E

③

                    A             B           C           D           E

④

                    A             B           C           D           E

⑤

                    A             B           C           D           E

## SUCCEED

Choose the figure on the right that is a rotation of the figure on the left.

**Example**

    **A**       **B**       **C**       **D**       **E**

Answer: **D**

**Now start the clock and do as many of these 15 questions as you can in 6 minutes.**

①

    **A**       **B**       **C**       **D**       **E**

②

    **A**       **B**       **C**       **D**       **E**

③

    **A**       **B**       **C**       **D**       **E**

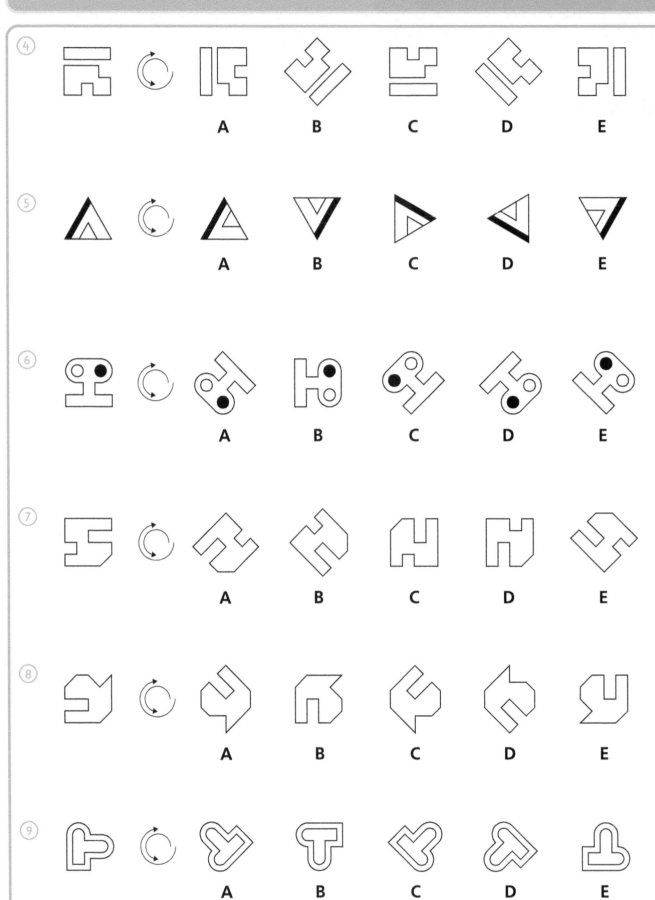

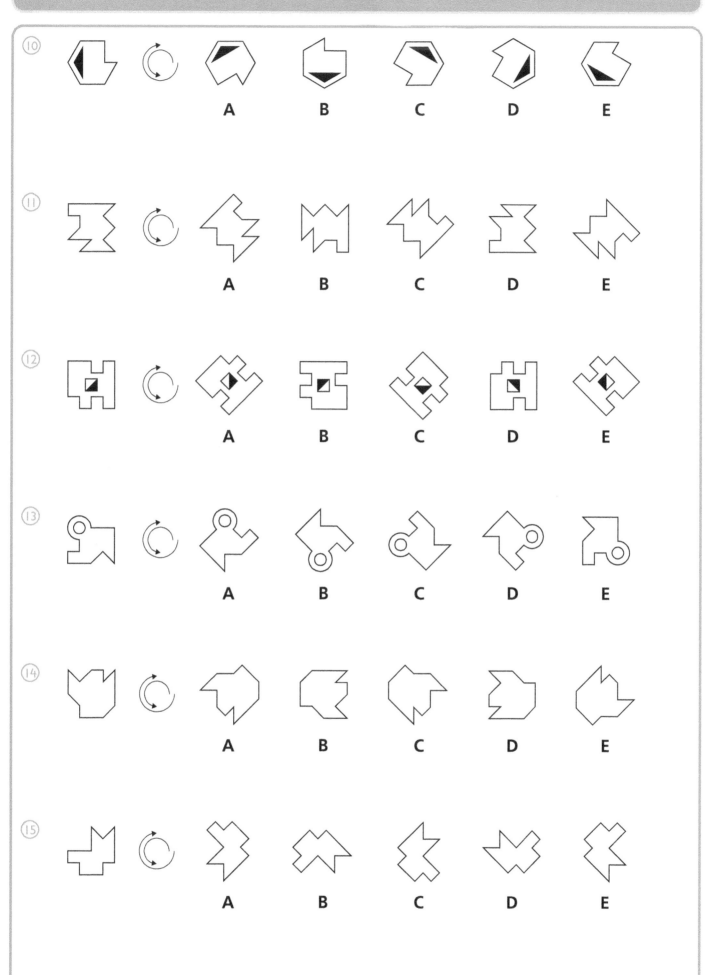

(10)

A   B   C   D   E

(11)

A   B   C   D   E

(12)

A   B   C   D   E

(13)

A   B   C   D   E

(14)

A   B   C   D   E

(15)

A   B   C   D   E

**THIS PAGE HAS DELIBERATELY
BEEN LEFT BLANK**

# LESSON 9:

# CUBES AND NETS

Look out for Billy's tips and hints.

# LEARN

In cubes and nets questions, you need to identify which cube can be formed from the net. A net is a flattened 2D outline of a 3D shape – it is the 3D shape unfolded. Nets may or may not have a picture on some of the faces. Each face must be matched exactly with a folded cube (or other 3D shape).

There are 11 different ways of folding up a net to form a cube, as shown below (the matching colours form opposite sides of the folded cube). Here we will be concentrating on techniques to help with this, sometimes challenging, question type.

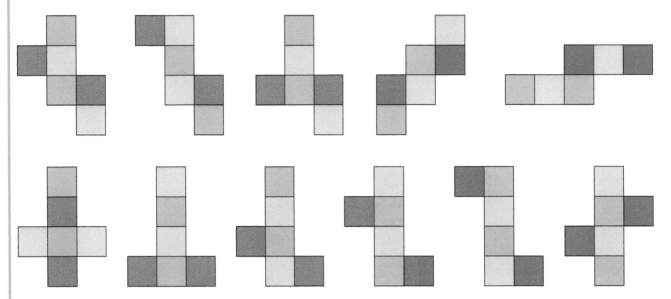

## Worked example

Look at the net below. Which of the cubes could be made from the net? Circle the letter under the correct answer option.

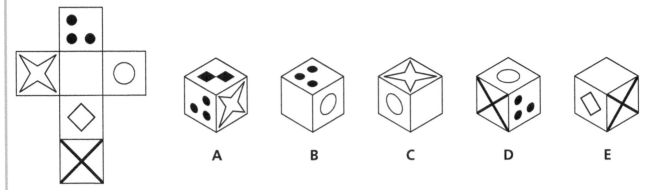

## Method

(1)     The cube net is one of the most common types of net you will find. First look to see if there are any pictures on the cubes that don't appear on the net. These pictures can be called 'aliens'. In this example, the upper face in option A shows two small black squares. These do not appear on the net so are 'aliens'. Therefore, you can eliminate option A.

(2)     When the net is folded, certain faces on the cube will be on the opposite side to each other. These faces can never be next to each other on the cubes. In the diagram below, faces of the same colour **can't** touch each other. Therefore, they can be eliminated. In this worked example, this will rule out options C and E.

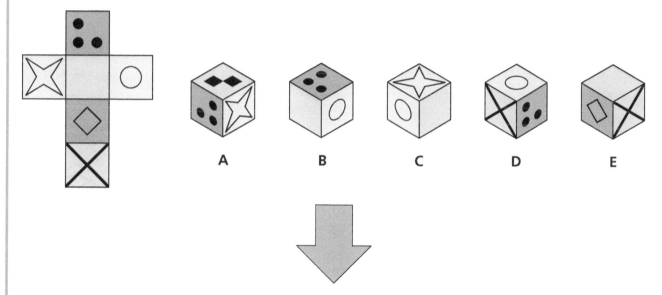

(3)     The next clue to look for is the 'alignment' of the pictures on the faces of the net. Often arrows or shapes that are asymmetrical can help you decide what the direction of the pictures should be on the folded cube. In this example, two of the three dots are aligned with the blank face. When folded, two dots will also be aligned with the face containing the star shape. Therefore, option D can be eliminated. This leaves option **B** as the only possible answer.

**Note:** Shapes on the faces of a net also create an 'L' shape when looked at together. When folded into a cube, they will sit next to each other. Therefore, you will never see three faces that are in a row on the net visible together on the cube.

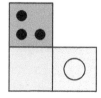

# DEVELOP

Look at each net. Which of the cubes could be made from the net? Circle the letter under the correct answer option.

①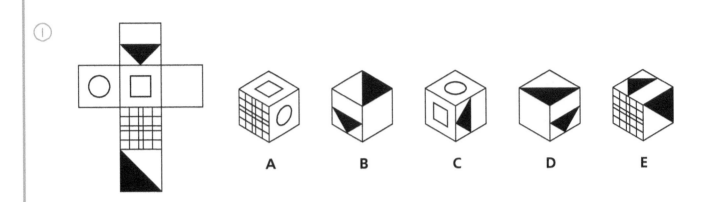

A    B    C    D    E

②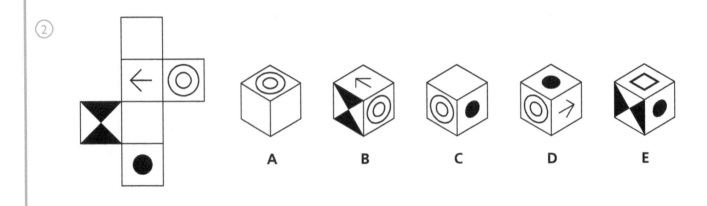

A    B    C    D    E

③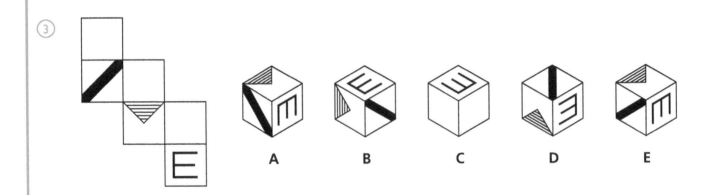

A    B    C    D    E

(4)

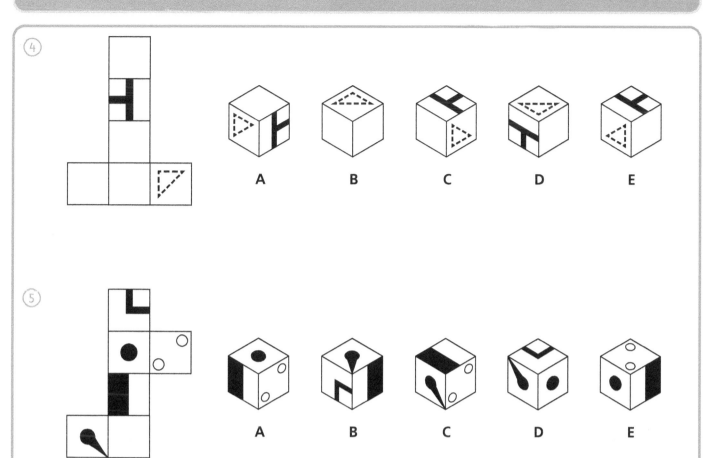

A  B  C  D  E

(5)

A  B  C  D  E

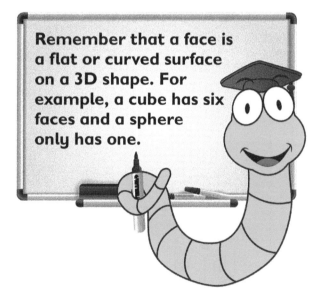

Remember that a face is a flat or curved surface on a 3D shape. For example, a cube has six faces and a sphere only has one.

# SUCCEED

Look at each net below. Which of the cubes could be made from the net? Circle the letter under the correct answer option.

**Example**

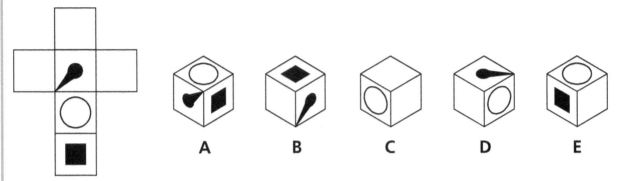

Answer: **E**

**Now start the clock and do as many of these 15 questions as you can in $7\frac{1}{2}$ minutes.**

①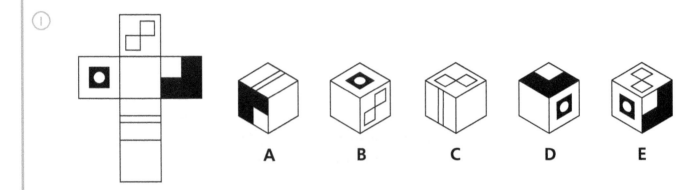

②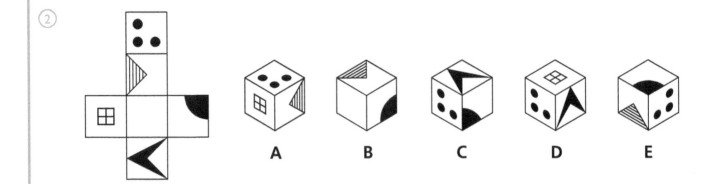

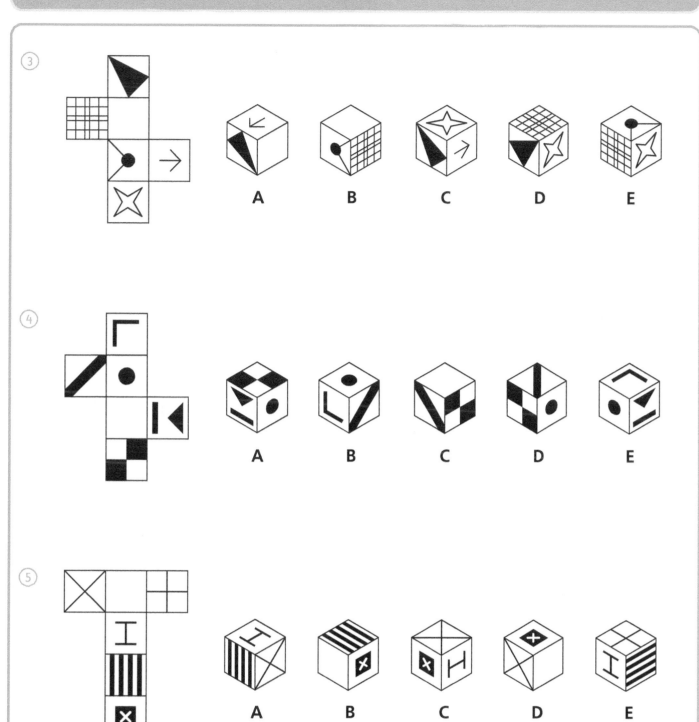

③

A     B     C     D     E

④

A     B     C     D     E

⑤

A     B     C     D     E

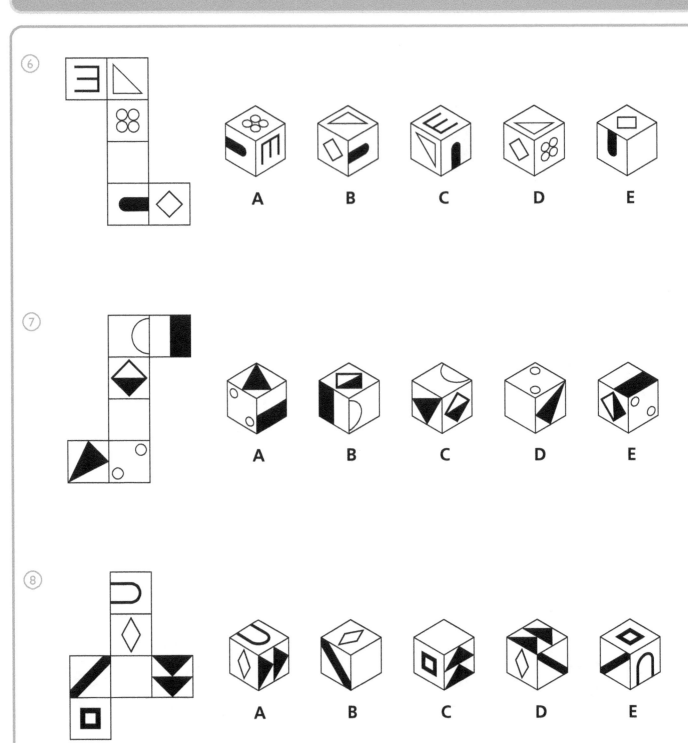

⑥

A    B    C    D    E

⑦

A    B    C    D    E

⑧

A    B    C    D    E

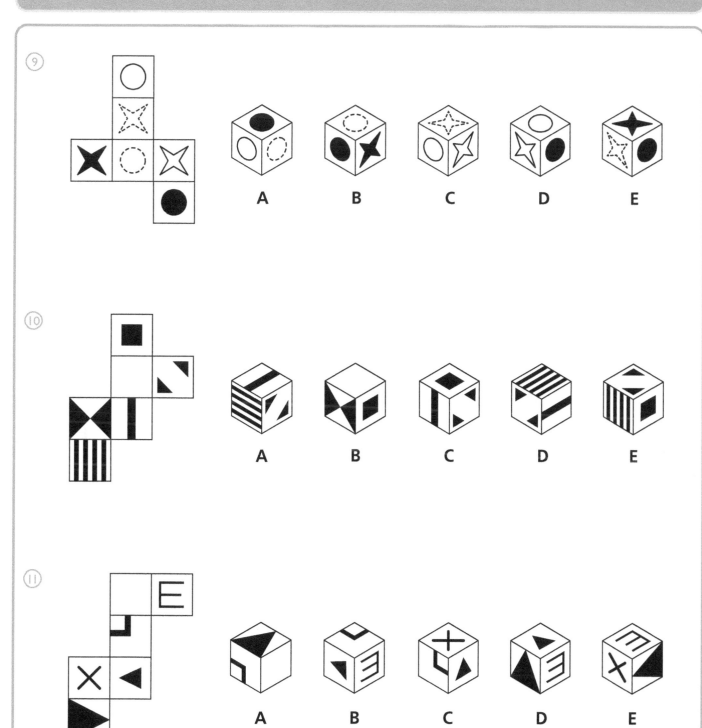

⑨  A  B  C  D  E

⑩  A  B  C  D  E

⑪  A  B  C  D  E

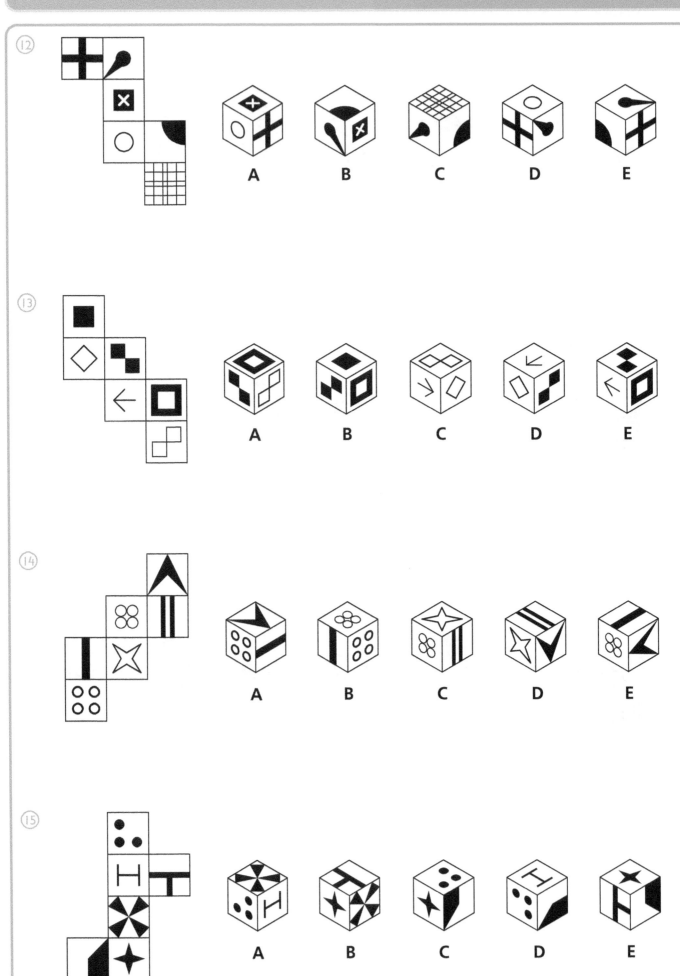

⑫

A    B    C    D    E

⑬

A    B    C    D    E

⑭

A    B    C    D    E

⑮

A    B    C    D    E

# LESSON 10:

# FOLD AND PUNCH

Look out for Billy's tips and hints.

# LEARN

This question type involves folding up a squared piece of paper, followed by punching holes through it, before imagining what it looks like unfolded. You will be shown the steps taken to fold up the square of paper at the top of the question. The number of steps can vary. The black arrow indicates the direction of the fold. Your task is to find the answer option that looks like the paper when it has been folded, punched and then unfolded.

Let's look at a worked example.

**Worked example**

Look at the square of paper, which is folded up and then has holes punched through it. Which answer option shows what the paper would look like when it is unfolded? Circle the letter below the correct answer.

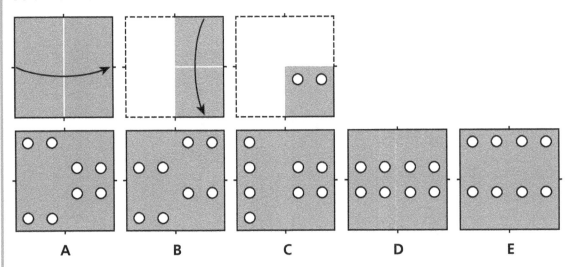

| A | B | C | D | E |

**Method**

(1)    Working backwards from the punched holes step-by-step can really help with these questions.

(2)    If you can write on the question paper in the exam, you can quickly draw where you believe the holes will appear when the paper is unfolded. See the diagrams below.

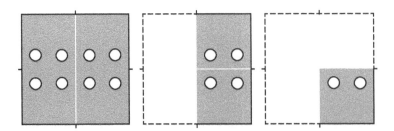

(3)    Using elimination will always help to limit the answer options in these questions.

(4)    Check that you have correctly considered how symmetry or reflection influence the answer. The answer is **D**.

## Fun task

Fold and punch activities can be fun to practise. Using sticky notes and a hole punch will reveal how the square paper will look after holes have been made and the paper unfolded. Have a go at doing the worked example using this equipment.

These questions are easier to solve if you work backwards from the final folded shape. Look carefully at each square and decide where there will be new holes.

# DEVELOP

Look at the square of paper, which is folded up and then has holes punched through it. Which answer option shows what the paper would look like when it is unfolded? Circle the letter below the correct answer.

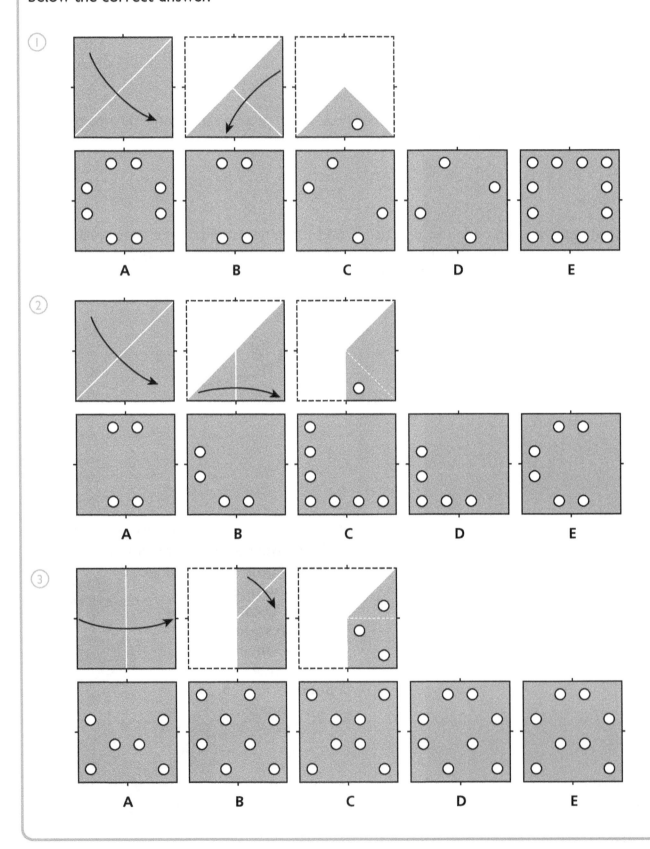

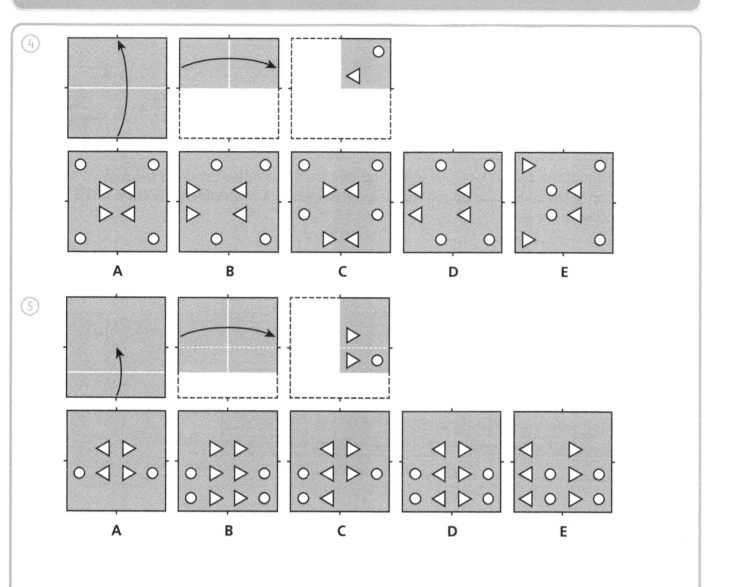

(4)

A    B    C    D    E

(5)

A    B    C    D    E

# SUCCEED

7:30
7½ minutes

Look at the square of paper, which is folded up and then has holes punched through it. Which answer option shows what the paper would look like when it is unfolded? Circle the letter below the correct answer.

**Example**

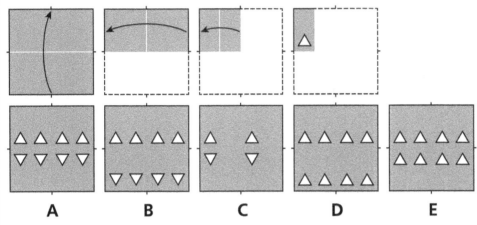

A    B    C    D    E

Answer: **A**

**Now start the clock and do as many of these 15 questions as you can in 7½ minutes.**

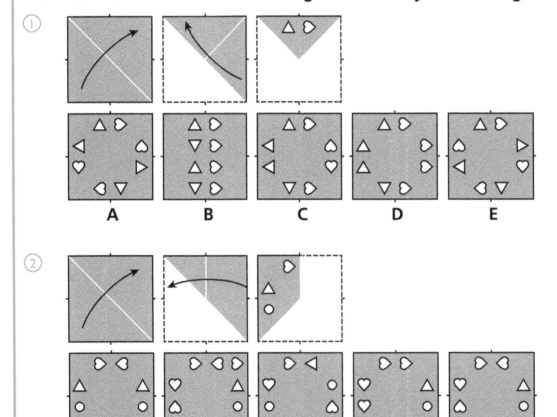

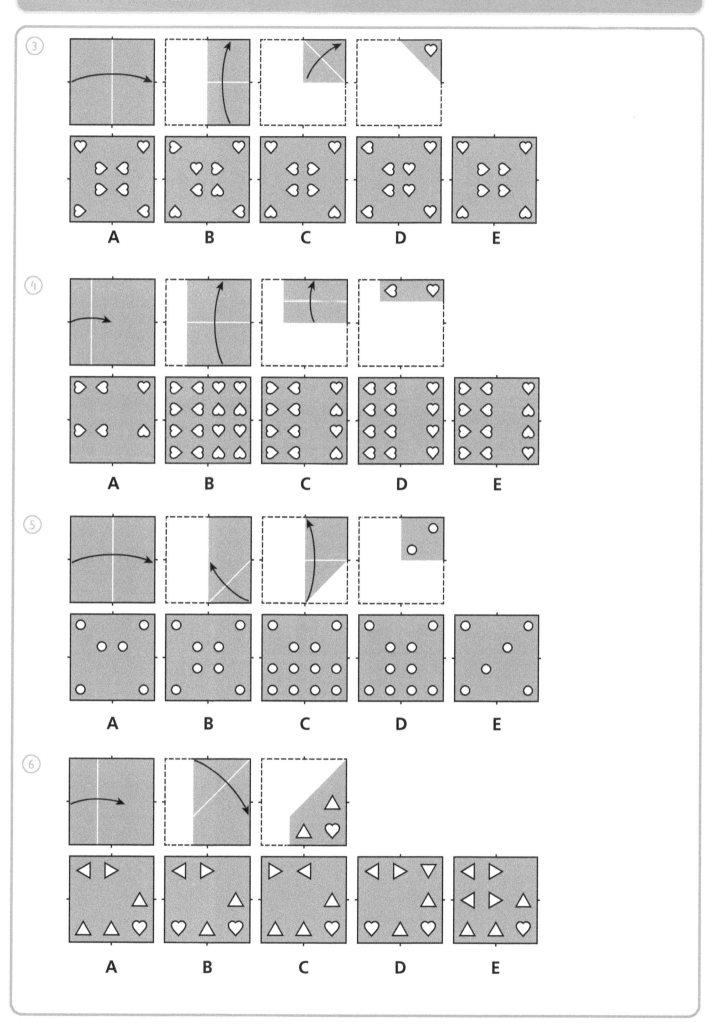

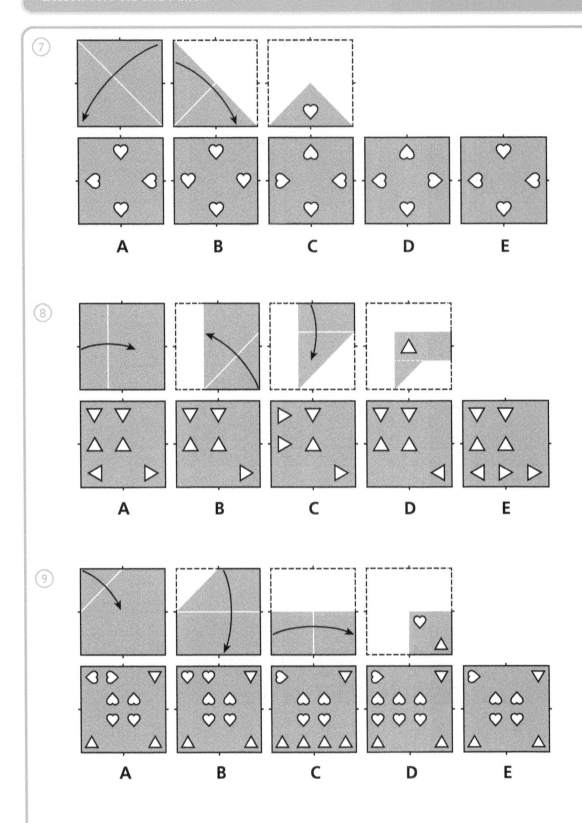

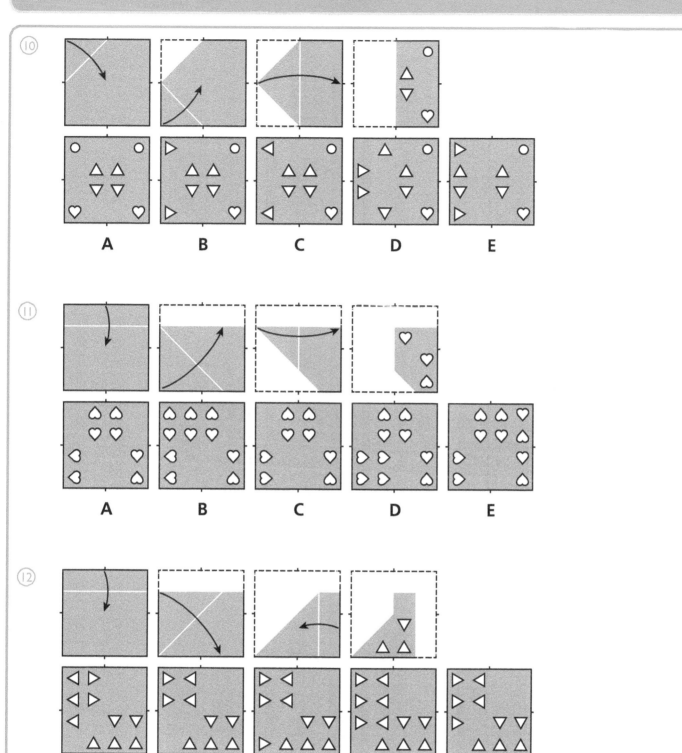

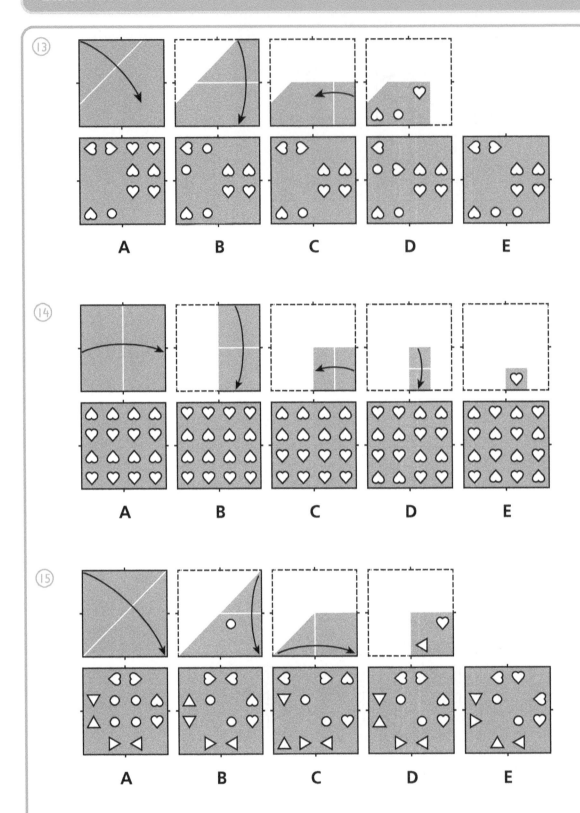

# LESSON 11:

# BLOCK COUNTING

Look out for Billy's tips and hints.

# LEARN

This type of spatial reasoning question involves counting the number of blocks in a pile. The blocks could be cube-shaped, cuboid-shaped, T-shaped or L-shaped. The blocks are always the same shape in any given diagram. Some of the blocks are not visible but they must be there to hold up the ones you can see. In other words, blocks cannot be suspended in thin air and they must be fully supported by blocks underneath.

**Worked example**

Select the answer that correctly shows how many blocks are in the diagram.

| 10 | 13 | 11 | 9 | 12 |
|----|----|----|---|----|
| A | B | C | D | E |

**Method**

(1)     First study the pile and understand how it has been compiled. Look at the different stacks and try to establish how many blocks high each one is.

(2)     In the example above, it is clear to see the stack at the back left of the pile is three blocks high. This can be written above the stack. Next to this are two blocks (only one is visible), followed by another two blocks. At the front of the pile are four single blocks.

(3)     Finally, add up the number of blocks. 3 + 2 + 2 + 4 = 11

The answer is therefore **C**.

## Warm-up task

*Number of blocks*

There are many jobs that require strong spatial reasoning skills, for example an engineer or architect. In the diagram below, which shows a set of stairs and a landing in a house, how many blocks can you count?

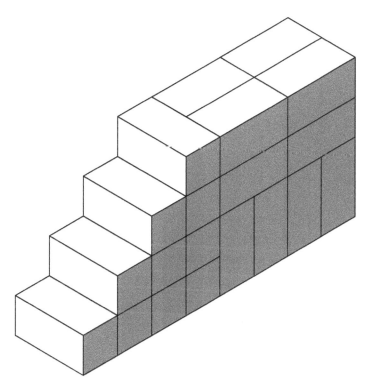

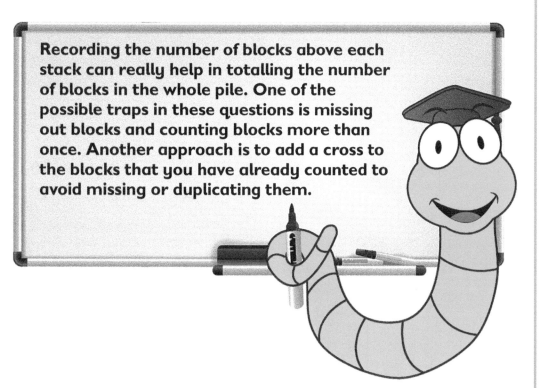

**Recording the number of blocks above each stack can really help in totalling the number of blocks in the whole pile. One of the possible traps in these questions is missing out blocks and counting blocks more than once. Another approach is to add a cross to the blocks that you have already counted to avoid missing or duplicating them.**

# DEVELOP

Now try these.

Select the answer which correctly shows how many blocks are in each diagram.

①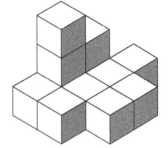

| 10 | 12 | 9 | 11 | 13 |
|----|----|---|----|----|
| A | B | C | D | E |

②

| 13 | 16 | 15 | 14 | 12 |
|----|----|----|----|----|
| A | B | C | D | E |

③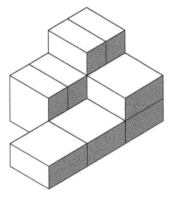

| 9 | 8 | 10 | 11 | 12 |
|---|---|----|----|----|
| A | B | C | D | E |

④

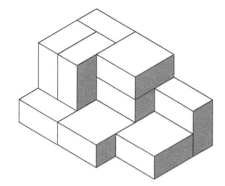

| 10 | 14 | 12 | 13 | 11 |
|----|----|----|----|----|
| A | B | C | D | E |

⑤

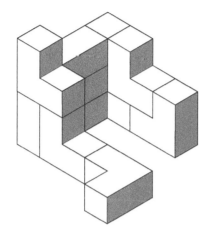

| 8 | 10 | 11 | 9 | 7 |
|---|----|----|---|---|
| A | B | C | D | E |

## SUCCEED

Select the answer that correctly shows how many blocks are in each diagram.

**Example**

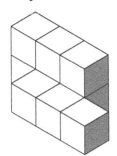

| 10 | 13 | 11 | 9 | 12 |
|----|----|----|----|----|
| A | B | C | D | E |

Answer: **D**

**Now start the clock and do as many of these 15 questions as you can in 7½ minutes.**

①

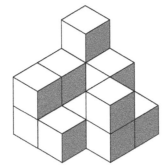

| 11 | 12 | 13 | 10 | 14 |
|----|----|----|----|----|
| A | B | C | D | E |

②

| 24 | 20 | 22 | 21 | 23 |
|----|----|----|----|----|
| A | B | C | D | E |

③

| 17 | 21 | 18 | 20 | 19 |
|----|----|----|----|----|
| A | B | C | D | E |

④

| 10 | 11 | 13 | 12 | 9 |
|----|----|----|----|---|
| A | B | C | D | E |

⑤

| 12 | 10 | 11 | 14 | 13 |
|----|----|----|----|----|
| A | B | C | D | E |

⑥

| 8 | 12 | 9 | 11 | 10 |
|---|----|---|----|----|
| A | B | C | D | E |

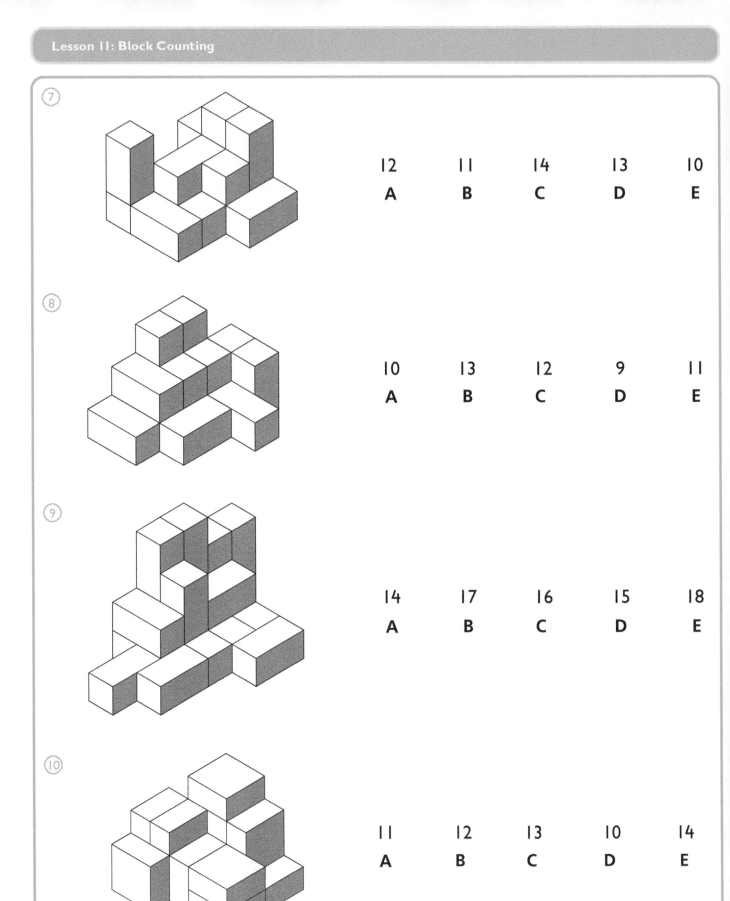

(7)

| 12 | 11 | 14 | 13 | 10 |
|----|----|----|----|----|
| A | B | C | D | E |

(8)

| 10 | 13 | 12 | 9 | 11 |
|----|----|----|----|----|
| A | B | C | D | E |

(9)

| 14 | 17 | 16 | 15 | 18 |
|----|----|----|----|----|
| A | B | C | D | E |

(10)

| 11 | 12 | 13 | 10 | 14 |
|----|----|----|----|----|
| A | B | C | D | E |

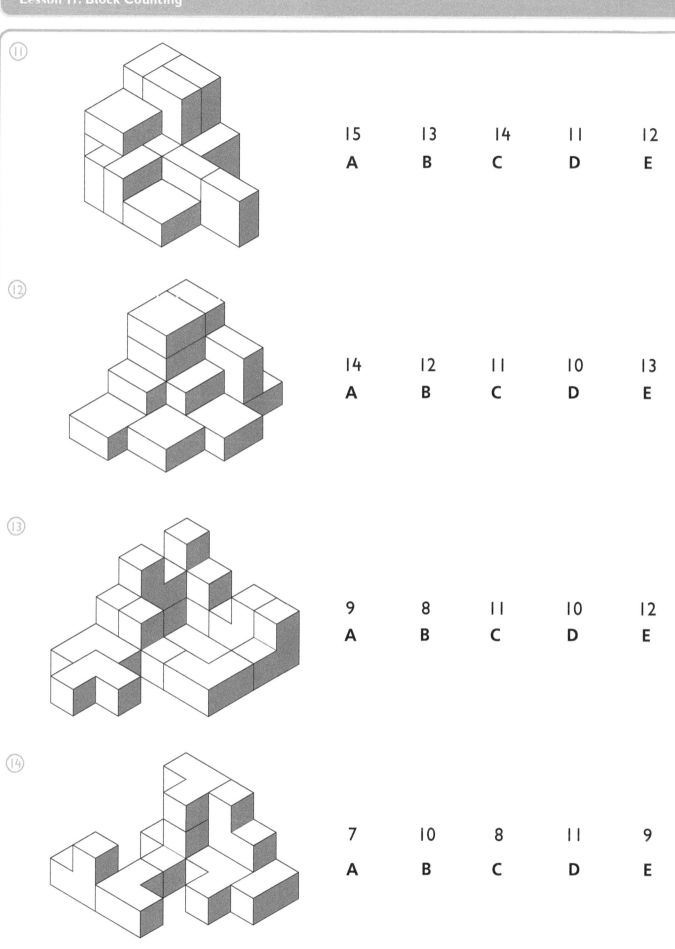

⑪

15  13  14  11  12
A   B   C   D   E

⑫

14  12  11  10  13
A   B   C   D   E

⑬

9   8   11  10  12
A   B   C   D   E

⑭

7   10  8   11  9
A   B   C   D   E

⑮

| 9 | 12 | 11 | 13 | 10 |
|---|----|----|----|----|
| A | B | C | D | E |

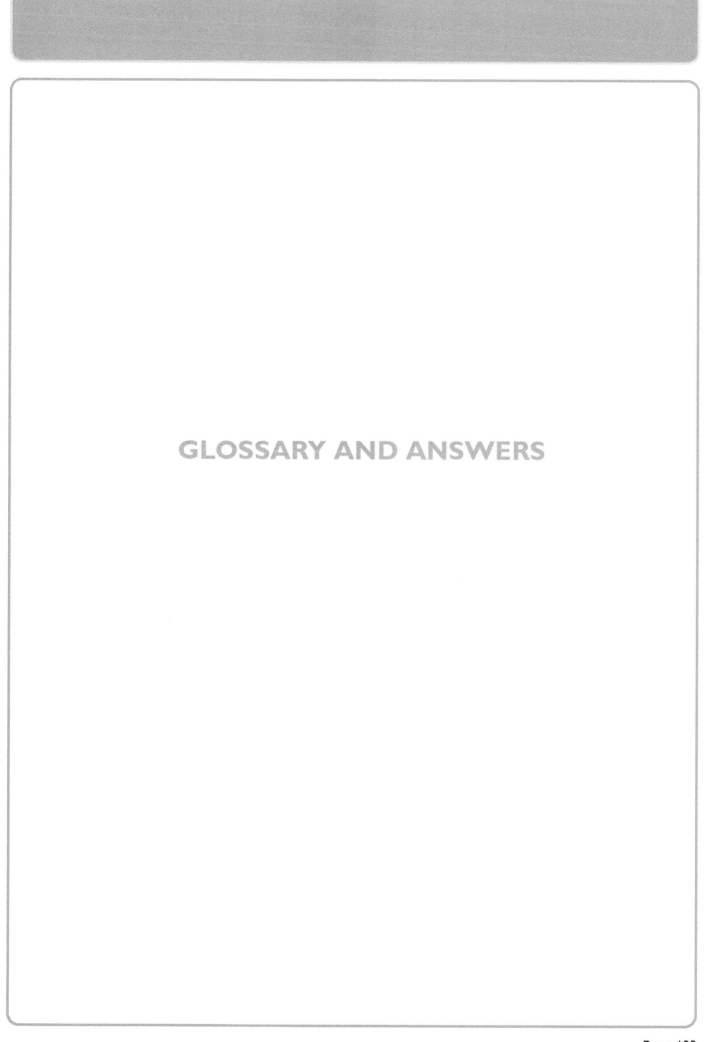

GLOSSARY AND ANSWERS

# Glossary

| Key term | Definition |
|---|---|
| Angle | The space between two intersecting lines. |
| Anti-clockwise | The opposite direction to the movement of the hands of a clock. |
| Clockwise | The direction in which the hands of a clock move. |
| Figure | A combination of shapes that work together to form one overall image. For example, in non-verbal reasoning, one single answer option is called a 'figure'. |
| Latin square format | An array filled with different symbols, each occurring exactly once in each row and exactly once in each column.<br><br>| A | B | C |<br>|---|---|---|<br>| C | A | B |<br>| B | C | A | |
| Layering | When a shape is in front of or behind another shape, or where two or more shapes overlap each other. |
| Line symmetry | A 2D shape has symmetry if a line can be drawn through it to show that one side of it is a reflection of the other. |
| Number | A quantity or amount, e.g. number of sides. |
| Overlapping | To cover a shape partly by going over its edge, or to cover part of the same shape. |
| Position | A place where a shape is located or has been drawn, e.g. top, middle or bottom of a box. |

| Reflection | A transformation in which a geometric figure is reflected across a line, creating a mirror image. |
|---|---|
| Rotation | A shape is rotated when it is turned around a fixed point. For example, the triangle below has been rotated. |
| Shading | The darkening of a shape with lines or block of colour, e.g.<br><br>hatched or grey |
| Size | The overall dimension or magnitude of a shape or figure. |

# Answers

## LESSON 1: CLASSES UNLIKE
### Develop (page 13)

| Question | Answer | Explanation |
|---|---|---|
| 1. | E | All the other figures have the same shading on the inner shape. |
| 2. | D | All the other figures have four lines. |
| 3. | D | In all the other figures, the smaller overlapping circles both have black shading inside the larger circle. |
| 4. | A | All the other figures have a dividing line in the centre that runs from a corner of the pentagon to the middle of the opposite side. |
| 5. | D | All the other figures contain a right-angled triangle. |

### Succeed (pages 14–16)

| Question | Answer | Explanation |
|---|---|---|
| 1. | E | Each figure should have four points on the star without a circle; E has five. |
| 2. | B | Each figure contains an even number of sides; B has an odd number, seven. |
| 3. | B | The arrows must enter the shape through a horizontal line of the shape. |
| 4. | A | Each figure has an exact, small black duplicate of the large shape inside it. |
| 5. | D | The square in the centre of the string of squares must have a cross fill whereby the ends of the lines meet the corners of the square. |
| 6. | E | Each large shape contains a black circle, a grey triangle and a white, four-sided shape. E has a white hexagon. |
| 7. | C | The line surrounding half the shape meets the shape and then circles it in a clockwise direction. C goes anti-clockwise. |
| 8. | B | Each figure has a line of horizontal symmetry, except B. |
| 9. | D | The small circle inside the shape matches the colour of the part of the larger circle overlapping the large shape. |
| 10. | D | If all shapes were rotated such that the triangle sits on the top left of the horizontal line and the circle beneath the line and to the right, in D the shapes would be the other way round. |
| 11. | A | Exactly one third of the other shapes is shaded. |
| 12. | C | Each figure consists of two identical shapes. In C, one shape is flipped. |
| 13. | C | Each figure has three segments shaded. In C, two segments are shaded. |
| 14. | A | The dashed line should always be applied to the middle shape. |
| 15. | E | Three identical shapes make the figure; the sizes are irrelevant. |

## LESSON 2: CLASSES ALIKE
### Develop (page 19)

| Question | Answer | Explanation |
|---|---|---|
| 1. | C | The 'spikes' or 'arms' belonging to the figure plus the small black shapes inside the large white shape add up to 8. |

| 2. | E | Inside the large shape, which is divided into four equal sections, there are three small shapes (which are the same in both figures) appearing in a clockwise direction: white circle, black triangle, cross shape. |
|---|---|---|
| 3. | A | In each figure there is one white circle, one triangle, one square and one small black circle that must appear inside one of the other shapes. |
| 4. | E | The number of lines matches the number of small shapes; one of which must be a white circle. |
| 5. | B | Each of the three figures is made from three triangles, one of which is shaded black. |

## Succeed (pages 20–22)

| Question | Answer | Explanation |
|---|---|---|
| 1. | A | The figures have ten sides in total. |
| 2. | B | Each figure has a black circle on top of a white rectangle on top of a grey triangle. |
| 3. | C | Each figure is made from a circle and a square. |
| 4. | D | Each figure has a vertical line of symmetry. |
| 5. | E | The square and triangle in each figure have a striped fill and a cross fill. |
| 6. | B | Each figure must contain two circles. |
| 7. | E | In each figure there is a curved shape inside a straight-sided shape. |
| 8. | C | The large, square-like shape contains a small square with a diagonal cross fill. |
| 9. | B | The grey area is over an obtuse angle. The black area can be over an acute or right-angled angle, not obtuse. |
| 10. | D | Eactly half of the shape is shaded. |
| 11. | D | Each figure has an even number of straight sides with a black circle inside. |
| 12. | B | The arrow in each figure points towards the white square. |
| 13. | E | Each figure has seven sides. |
| 14. | C | Each figure is made from one continuous curved line. |
| 15. | A | Each figure has a white central circle, a black triangle at one end of the string and a square with a cross fill at the other end. |

## LESSON 3: SERIES

### Learn: warm-up task (page 24)

E

### Develop (page 26)

| Question | Answer | Explanation |
|---|---|---|
| 1. | E | Moving left to right, the black circle moves one corner clockwise around the square.<br>The central square rotates 45° and becomes larger in each figure. |

| 2. | C | A repeating alternate pattern moving from left to right. The figure will be the same as in the second square. |
| 3. | B | The shapes increase by one more side moving from left to right. |
| 4. | A | The pattern is alternating. Therefore, moving from left to right, the first square would be the same as the third square. |

## Succeed (pages 27–30)

| Question | Answer | Explanation |
| --- | --- | --- |
| 1. | C | One hexagon changes to a circle each time in a clockwise direction. |
| 2. | B | From left to right, the small white square moves in an anti-clockwise direction. The black circle rotates 72° clockwise. |
| 3. | E | The white square moves from the top left corner of the box to the bottom right. The black circle moves down the box and then up again and the cross moves from the top right to the bottom left corner of the box. |
| 4. | B | The shape flips on the horizontal, box to box and gradually 'fills' with the shade. |
| 5. | C | The large shape rotates 90° clockwise and the smaller, thick-lined shape rotates 135° clockwise. |
| 6. | D | The circle at the bottom right of the string moves to the top left and the rest shift down each time. |
| 7. | A | The shaded area of the figure grows in size each time. The white shape grows in length each time and gains another black circle. The whole figure rotates 90° anti-clockwise. |
| 8. | A | The vertical line loses one short horizontal line and the large 'C' shape gains one long horizontal line each time. The figure flips on the vertical. |
| 9. | A | From left to right, the figure loses one 'arm' from the white shape in an anti-clockwise direction and another black circle is added in a clockwise direction each time. |
| 10. | B | The white circle rotates 45° anti-clockwise inside the octagon. The grey triangles rotate 45° clockwise. The black triangle rotates 90° clockwise. |
| 11. | C | The cross with the black triangle rotates 135° anti-clockwise and the white arrow rotates 135° clockwise. |
| 12. | E | The long black segment and the small black triangle in the centre rotate around the square 90° clockwise. A small grey square is added each time in an anti-clockwise direction. |
| 13. | D | The small white circle alternates position between top left and bottom right of the box. The white rectangle moves up the box incrementally and the black triangle moves down and back up the box. |
| 14. | D | The hexagon changes line style every three boxes. The circle rotates 90° anti-clockwise from left to right. |
| 15. | E | The diagonal line in the top right of the box moves to the left. The next diagonal line down, and the next one down on the far left, remain in place. The fourth diagonal line down alternates between two positions as does the bottom diagonal line. |

## LESSON 4: ANALOGIES
### Learn: warm-up task (pages 32–33)
B; D; B

### Develop (page 35)

| Question | Answer | Explanation |
|---|---|---|
| 1. | B | The square is divided in half. Moving from left to right, the two halves of shading swaps. |
| 2. | B | Moving from left to right, the shapes move one place clockwise. |
| 3. | B | Moving from left to right, the figure increases by one side and an extra dashed line is added to the middle. |
| 4. | C | Moving from left to right, all the shapes are a mirror image of the opposite side. |

### Succeed (pages 36–38)

| Question | Answer | Explanation |
|---|---|---|
| 1. | B | The figure flips on the vertical and the shape takes the style of the vertical line, which disappears. |
| 2. | A | The large shape rotates 90° and the shading from the small shapes goes to the opposite half of the large shape. |
| 3. | E | The inner large shape rotates 90°, gains an extra part to it and takes its line style from the large shape that disappears. The smaller shapes enter the opposite ends of the rotated shape. |
| 4. | C | The upper right shape flips on the horizontal and becomes the largest shape. The upper left shape rotates 45° and becomes the second largest shape. The lower shape flips on the horizontal and becomes the smallest shape. |
| 5. | C | The shapes swap size and position but retain shading style. |
| 6. | B | The figure rotates 180°, loses one 'arm' of the shape and is shaded grey. |
| 7. | D | The figure flips on the horizontal, the large shape outline becomes dashed and the inner shape becomes black. |
| 8. | E | The line style in the upper right part of the figure is applied to the small lower left shape and becomes larger. The lower left line style is applied to the upper right shape and this shape enters the other larger shape. |
| 9. | B | The large open shape in the centre of the figure flips on the horizontal and takes a thick line style. The two smaller shapes flip on the horizontal, merge and take the shading from the rectangle. |
| 10. | B | The outer half-shape duplicates, creating a whole shape. The inner shape and its cross fill swap line styles. |
| 11. | E | The upper shape in the figure rotates 90° anti-clockwise and is positioned on top of an enlarged lower shape. The shapes swap shading. |
| 12. | D | The large shape duplicates and rotates 180° about the centre of the small central shape. |

| 13. | C | The outer parts of the figure enlarge and merge to form a shape. The small central shape enlarges, takes the shading of the square (which disappears) and enters the new large shape. |
| 14. | E | The small shapes on the outside of the grid enter the box one place anti-clockwise to its current position and the whole figure enlarges. |
| 15. | A | The figure flips on the vertical. The large shape takes its outline from the horizontal line inside it. The lower figure enters the shape, taking its shading from the upper rectangle. |

## LESSON 5: MATRICES

### Learn: warm-up task (page 41)

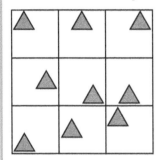

### Develop (pages 42–43)

| Question | Answer | Explanation |
|---|---|---|
| 1. | E | Moving diagonally across the matrix from top left to bottom right, the figures are the same in each diagonal line (circle, triangle or square). Moving diagonally across the matrix from top right to bottom left, the shading is consistent in each diagonal line (horizontal stripes, black shading and diagonal shading). |
| 2. | D | The black square moves clockwise 90° around the grid. |
| 3. | A | Moving along each row from left to right, the curved line and bisecting line move 90° clockwise. The straight bisecting line alternates between being dashed and solid in each figure along each row. |
| 4. | B | Looking diagonally at the matrix from top left to bottom right, the shading in each diagonal is consistent. Moving from left to right along each row, the number of sides in each figure increases by one. |
| 5. | E and D | In each vertical column, the figures are identical. |
| 6. | A and E | The shapes are arranged in a diagonal line from top right to bottom left. |

### Succeed (pages 44–47)

| Question | Answer | Explanation |
|---|---|---|
| 1. | C | The figures reflect across the grid and the shapes swap shading. |
| 2. | E | The figures rotate 90° clockwise down the grid and the shapes swap line style. |

| 3. | B | From left to right, the small centre shape goes from one to three shapes in a line and take their shading from the upper shape. The upper and lower shapes swap positions and the new bottom shape takes the shading from the original bottom shape. |
| 4. | A | The shapes reflect diagonally and the shading rotates 90°. |
| 5. | D | From left to right, the arrow moves 90° clockwise and the square moves 135° clockwise. |
| 6. | C | From left to right, the figure rotates 90° clockwise and the line style of the 'Z' shape becomes dotted. |
| 7. | D | From left to right, the lower shape becomes the largest. Inside this come the upper left shape and then the upper right shape is the smallest. The two upper shapes swap shading. |
| 8. | E | The large shape on the left duplicates and reflects on the vertical, merging to become one large shape. It takes the shading from the upper right square and the small, lower shape enlarges and enters it. |
| 9. | A | The matrix is an overall pattern. |
| 10. | D | The small shapes are set in a Latin square format where only one shape appears in one row and one column. The larger shapes are also set in a Latin square format. |
| 11. | C | Where the shapes in the top and second rows merge and overlap, that area becomes a black shape in the bottom row. |
| 12. | B | The shapes are the same across rows and rotate 90° clockwise each time. The shading of the shapes is in a Latin square format. |
| 13. | C | The large shapes are the same across rows and rotate 90° clockwise from left to right. The small shapes are the same down the columns and move 90° anti-clockwise around the boxes each time. |
| 14. | E | The direction of the arrows is set in a Latin square format and the number of rectangles is also set in a Latin square format. |
| 15. | D | The small shapes are the same down the columns. The large shapes are set in a Latin square format and the outer line style of the shapes is also set in a Latin square format. |

## LESSON 6: HORIZONTAL AND VERTICAL CODES
### Learn: warm-up task (page 51)
SG

### Develop (page 52)

| Question | Answer | Explanation |
| --- | --- | --- |
| 1. | B | RST stands for the number of shaded dots and FGH stands for the type of shape at the top of the boxes. |
| 2. | D | XYZ stands for the orientation of the 'L' shape and LMN stands for the shading of the 'L' shape. |
| 3. | E | FGHK stands for the type of large shape and XYZ stands for the number of shapes. |

| 4. | C | LM stands for the number of small black shapes, RS stands for the type of large shape and FGH stands for the type of small shape. |
| 5. | A | XY stands for the position of the black triangle, (i.e. inside or outside the large shape), FG stands for the type of shading on the right side of the large shape and LMN stands for the type of large shape. |

## Succeed (pages 53–56)

| Question | Answer | Explanation |
|----------|--------|-------------|
| 1. | D | RST stands for the upper small shape and KLMN stands for the type of large shape. |
| 2. | E | FGH stands for the small black shape and XYZ stands for the large shape. |
| 3. | A | LMN stands for the type of large shape and RST stands for the shading of the large shape. |
| 4. | C | XYZ stands for the position of the circle (top, bottom, middle of box) and FGH stands for the shading of the circle. |
| 5. | B | KLMN stands for the line style of the square and RST stands for the position of the circle (outside, overlapping or inside the square). |
| 6. | D | RST stands for the number of circles inside the large shape and WXYZ stands for overall number of small shapes. |
| 7. | C | XYZ stands for the amount of the rectangle that is shaded and FGH stands for the position of the arrow. |
| 8. | B | LM stands for the direction of the arrow, RST stands for the number of squares and FG stands for the shading of the squares. |
| 9. | E | RST stands for the type of small shape, LM stands for the shading of the small shape and XY stands for the inner line style of the large shape. |
| 10. | C | FG stands for the number of black dots, ST stands for the type of vertical line on the right of the figure and LMN stands for the shape to the left of the figure. |
| 11. | A | LMN stands for the type of large shape, XY stands for the type of small shape and FG stands for the number of small shapes. |
| 12. | D | RST stands for the position of the circle (inside, overlapping or outside of the large shape), LMN stands for the line style of the large shape and WXYZ stands for the type of large shape. |
| 13. | E | XYZ stands for the position of the horizontal line within the triangle shape, FGH stands for the shading above the horizontal line in the triangle shape and LMN stands for the number of small triangles. |
| 14. | C | FGH stands for the position of the arrowhead on the horizontal line, RST stands for the number of thick vertical lines and LMN stands for the type of large shape. |
| 15. | B | KLM stands for the position of the black arrow, PQRS stands for the line style of the large circle and FGH stands for the position of the white arrow. |

# LESSON 7: SHAPE COMPLETION
## Develop (page 61)

| Question | Answer |
| --- | --- |
| 1. | D |
| 2. | C |
| 3. | B |
| 4. | D |
| 5. | E |

## Succeed (pages 62–64)

| Question | Answer |
| --- | --- |
| 1. | C |
| 2. | E |
| 3. | B |
| 4. | A |
| 5. | D |
| 6. | B |
| 7. | E |
| 8. | D |
| 9. | C |
| 10. | A |
| 11. | C |
| 12. | E |
| 13. | E |
| 14. | B |
| 15. | C |

# LESSON 8: ROTATION
## Learn: warm-up task (page 67)

| Shape | Rotated 45° | Rotated 90° | Rotated 135° | Rotated 180° |
| --- | --- | --- | --- | --- |
| | | | | |

## Develop (page 68)

| Question | Answer | Explanation |
| --- | --- | --- |
| 1. | C | The correct answer has been rotated 135° clockwise. |
| 2. | D | The correct answer has been rotated 180°. |
| 3. | B | The correct answer has been rotated 135° clockwise. |
| 4. | E | The correct answer has been rotated 135° clockwise. |
| 5. | C | The correct answer has been rotated 180°. |

## Succeed (pages 69–71)

| Question | Answer |
| --- | --- |
| 1. | B |
| 2. | C |
| 3. | A |
| 4. | E |
| 5. | B |
| 6. | D |
| 7. | E |
| 8. | C |
| 9. | A |
| 10. | D |
| 11. | C |
| 12. | E |
| 13. | B |
| 14. | C |
| 15. | E |

## LESSON 9: CUBES AND NETS
### Develop (pages 76–77)

| Question | Answer |
| --- | --- |
| 1. | C |
| 2. | C |
| 3. | E |
| 4. | A |
| 5. | D |

### Succeed (pages 78–82)

| Question | Answer |
| --- | --- |
| 1. | A |
| 2. | C |
| 3. | D |

| | |
|---|---|
| 4. | E |
| 5. | D |
| 6. | B |
| 7. | C |
| 8. | A |
| 9. | D |
| 10. | E |
| 11. | B |
| 12. | B |
| 13. | E |
| 14. | A |
| 15. | C |

## LESSON 10: FOLD AND PUNCH
### Develop (pages 86–87)

| Question | Answer |
|---|---|
| 1. | C |
| 2. | B |
| 3. | E |
| 4. | A |
| 5. | D |

### Succeed (pages 88–92)

| Question | Answer |
|---|---|
| 1. | A |
| 2. | E |
| 3. | C |
| 4. | C |
| 5. | B |
| 6. | A |
| 7. | D |
| 8. | B |
| 9. | E |
| 10. | B |
| 11. | C |
| 12. | E |
| 13. | C |
| 14. | A |
| 15. | D |

## LESSON 11: BLOCK COUNTING
### Learn: warm-up task (page 95)
26 blocks

### Develop (pages 96–97)

| Question | Answer | Explanation |
|----------|--------|-------------|
| 1. | B | There are two hidden blocks. |
| 2. | C | There are two hidden blocks. |
| 3. | A | There is one hidden block. |
| 4. | E | There are two hidden blocks. |
| 5. | D | There are no hidden blocks; a part of all the blocks can be seen. |

### Succeed (pages 98–102)

| Question | Answer |
|----------|--------|
| 1. | E |
| 2. | A |
| 3. | D |
| 4. | B |
| 5. | E |
| 6. | D |
| 7. | A |
| 8. | C |
| 9. | B |
| 10. | C |
| 11. | A |
| 12. | E |
| 13. | D |
| 14. | E |
| 15. | C |

**THIS PAGE HAS DELIBERATELY
BEEN LEFT BLANK**

## Marking Chart

Fill in the boxes below with your results from the timed test in each Succeed section.

**Lesson 1: Classes Unlike** /15

**Lesson 2: Classes Alike** /15

**Lesson 3: Series** /15

**Lesson 4: Analogies** /15

**Lesson 5: Matrices** /15

**Lesson 6: Horizontal and Vertical Codes** /15

**Lesson 7: Shape Completion** /15

**Lesson 8: Rotation** /15

**Lesson 9: Cubes and Nets** /15

**Lesson 10: Fold and Punch** /15

**Lesson 11: Block Counting** /15

# Progress Grid

Colour these charts with your score from each Succeed section to see how well you have done.

## Lesson 1: Classes Unlike

| 1 | 2 | 3 | 4 | 5 | 6 | 7 | 8 | 9 | 10 | 11 | 12 | 13 | 14 | 15 |
|---|---|---|---|---|---|---|---|---|----|----|----|----|----|----|

## Lesson 2: Classes Alike

| 1 | 2 | 3 | 4 | 5 | 6 | 7 | 8 | 9 | 10 | 11 | 12 | 13 | 14 | 15 |
|---|---|---|---|---|---|---|---|---|----|----|----|----|----|----|

## Lesson 3: Series

| 1 | 2 | 3 | 4 | 5 | 6 | 7 | 8 | 9 | 10 | 11 | 12 | 13 | 14 | 15 |
|---|---|---|---|---|---|---|---|---|----|----|----|----|----|----|

## Lesson 4: Analogies

| 1 | 2 | 3 | 4 | 5 | 6 | 7 | 8 | 9 | 10 | 11 | 12 | 13 | 14 | 15 |
|---|---|---|---|---|---|---|---|---|----|----|----|----|----|----|

## Lesson 5: Matrices

| 1 | 2 | 3 | 4 | 5 | 6 | 7 | 8 | 9 | 10 | 11 | 12 | 13 | 14 | 15 |
|---|---|---|---|---|---|---|---|---|----|----|----|----|----|----|

## Lesson 6: Horizontal and Vertical Codes

| 1 | 2 | 3 | 4 | 5 | 6 | 7 | 8 | 9 | 10 | 11 | 12 | 13 | 14 | 15 |
|---|---|---|---|---|---|---|---|---|----|----|----|----|----|----|

## Lesson 7: Shape Completion

| 1 | 2 | 3 | 4 | 5 | 6 | 7 | 8 | 9 | 10 | 11 | 12 | 13 | 14 | 15 |
|---|---|---|---|---|---|---|---|---|----|----|----|----|----|----|

## Lesson 8: Rotation

| 1 | 2 | 3 | 4 | 5 | 6 | 7 | 8 | 9 | 10 | 11 | 12 | 13 | 14 | 15 |
|---|---|---|---|---|---|---|---|---|----|----|----|----|----|----|

## Lesson 9: Cubes and Nets

| 1 | 2 | 3 | 4 | 5 | 6 | 7 | 8 | 9 | 10 | 11 | 12 | 13 | 14 | 15 |
|---|---|---|---|---|---|---|---|---|----|----|----|----|----|----|

## Lesson 10: Fold and Punch

| 1 | 2 | 3 | 4 | 5 | 6 | 7 | 8 | 9 | 10 | 11 | 12 | 13 | 14 | 15 |
|---|---|---|---|---|---|---|---|---|----|----|----|----|----|----|

## Lesson 11: Block Counting

| 1 | 2 | 3 | 4 | 5 | 6 | 7 | 8 | 9 | 10 | 11 | 12 | 13 | 14 | 15 |
|---|---|---|---|---|---|---|---|---|----|----|----|----|----|----|

Read the statements below for some hints and tips.

**1–5:** Re-read the Learn section and have another go at the Develop questions.

**6–10:** Good effort! Re-try the questions you got wrong or didn't answer.

**11–15:** Well done! Keep up the good work.

# Notes